Radiant New York

Beauties

VALORI WELLS

14 PAPER-PIECED QUILT PROJECTS

C&T PUBLISHING

Editor-in-Chief: Darra Williamson

Editor: Candie Frankel

Technical Editors: Candie Frankel, Gailen Runge

Proofreader: Eva Simoni Erb

Cover Designer: Christina Jarumay

Book Designer: Adriane Bosworth

Design Director: Diane Pedersen

Illustrator: Tim Manibusan

Production Assistant: Jeff Carrillo

Photography: Valori Wells

Front cover: *Carnival Beauty*

Back cover: *Red Licorice, Radiant Beauty, Joshua Tree*

Published by C&T Publishing, Inc., P.O. Box 1456, Lafayette, California 94549

Library of Congress Cataloging-in-Publication Data

Wells, Valori.
    Radiant New York beauties : 14 paper-pieced quilt projects / Valori Wells.
        p. cm.
    ISBN 1-57120-199-8
    1. Patchwork--Patterns. 2. Quilting--Patterns. 3. Quilts--New York (State) I. Title.
    TT835 .W47848 2003
    746.46'041--dc21

                                    2002152913

Printed in China.
10 9 8 7 6 5 4 3 2 1

Top left: A sea urchin shell exhibits beautiful texture and a subtle radiating design.
Above and below: The points in a New York Beauty block mimic the protruding stems and circular motion of a handmade pussy willow wreath.

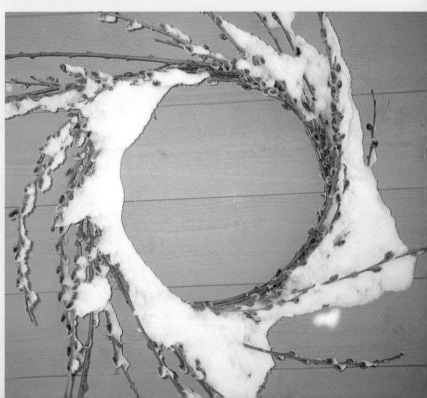

Dedication

This book is dedicated to all my quilting "Mothers." Working in this wonderful industry, I have met amazing, inspiring women who have changed my life. They have given me encouraging words and unconditional love and support. Through them, I have faith in myself to do anything I set my mind to.

And for those "Mothers" who don't quilt but who admire the art, thanks! My love goes out to these women whom I am lucky to have in my life.

This page: Looking directly into the centers of plants, cones, and flowers often yields great inspiration for radiating block designs.

Acknowledgments

I wish to acknowledge the following people who have made *Radiant New York Beauties* such a great book.

- My sewing fairies—Barbara, Betsy, Carolyn, Mom, Katrina, and Patricia. In addition to hours of sewing, they gave me encouragement and emotional support. I couldn't have made it without them.

- Todd Hensley, for believing in me, and the C&T family—especially Diane Pedersen, Christina Jarumay, and Tim Manibusan—for their skills and expertise in creating this book.

- Candie Frankel, the amazing developmental editor for *Radiant New York Beauties*, for all of her time, devotion, vision, and support.

- Adriane Bosworth, my book designer, who did a wonderful job interpreting my ideas to make the book both visually appealing and informative.

- All of my family at the Stitchin' Post, for seeing me through stressful days and just for being there.

- John, my amazing step-dad, who always believed in me even when I didn't. He brought me food when I was famished and wine when the day was over.

- Zoe, who once a month relieved my sore muscles with a great massage and eased my mind with insightful words.

Above: Two plant close-ups suggest an extraordinary variety of greens ranging across the spectrum from blue-green to yellow-green. *Below:* Interpreting blues and greens in a quilt palette.

Foreword

Those of us who are around when Valori arrives with a new quilt in tow know enough to take a big deep breath in preparation. We get a glimpse of what's in store just by eyeing the quilt back—the exposed quilting is a teaser as we wait for her to unfurl her latest creation.

Needless to say, Val went well beyond all our expectations when she completed the designs for her book of New York Beauties. Her interpretation of the fundamental aspects of radiating points in *Joshua Tree* is just a hint of where the art can take her.

Val's genius is revealed in her combination of design and fabric choices and confirmed with her machine quilting. All of her designs have a huge *aah!* factor. As each block goes together, the excitement builds. Once the quilt is fully assembled, the collective oohs and aahs can be heard throughout the room.

It is always so much fun to walk into The Stitchin' Post and see Val stacking bolts of fabrics on the cutting table. Her palette doesn't know any of the limits that we tend to place on ourselves. How many times have I spied Val's stack and thought, "Okay, this time she is going too far," only to eat my words a few weeks later.

The gift Val gives us in this collection is the freedom to leave our comfort zone—or not! She has designed quilts that run the gamut, from traditional to beyond contemporary, and allows us to choose for ourselves. The added beauty is that you can make her designs your own just by throwing in that favorite fabric.

All of Val's quilts are perfect backdrops for the fun, whimsical machine quilting that has become her trademark. Val has inspired a real quilting frenzy with her continuous-line motifs—spirals, flowers, leaves intertwining with circular twirls. Half the fun of looking at Val's quilts is seeing the incredible thread work in her machine quilting.

Too many quilters have somehow convinced themselves that New York Beauties are beyond their capabilities. As you peruse Val's book, keep in mind that many of us were neophytes when she asked us to help her. If we can do it, so can you! Paper piecing is the key to creating those perfect points.

You are in for a treat as you make your way through *Radiant New York Beauties.* The colors and fabric designs combine to create one radiant point after another. Val's creativity has always been infectious. It is such a pleasure to see her share her vision with the ever-expanding quilting community.

Betsy Mennesson

Table of Contents

Introduction

New York Beauty quilts have always fascinated me. The circular shapes and precise points draw me in and start me thinking of other design possibilities. I can remember two such quilts in my mother's book, *Memorabilia Quilting*, that set my creative mind working. Playing with color and pattern in a quilt design is a challenge that I love.

Four years ago, I returned to Sisters, Oregon, to join the family business, The Stitchin' Post. I enrolled in a New York Beauty class that my mother, Jean Wells, was teaching. She taught us how to paper-piece the arcs to get perfect points and how to sew curved seams. It wasn't nearly as hard as I thought it would be. Once I had mastered the stitching techniques, I was off and running with design ideas of my own. With the deadline for our annual store challenge fast approaching, I jumped in with both feet and designed the original block for *Radiant Beauty*. What a liberating experience! Playing with color and pattern then became the focus. I love how the quilt turned out.

More ideas for New York Beauty blocks soon began to fill my design journal. One thing led to another, and I kept making quilts with different blocks. I have enough blocks drafted to be making New York Beauties for years.

The intricate-looking arcs in New York Beauty blocks are made with paper-piecing patterns. Stitching directly on the paper pattern ensures perfect points every time. The paper is torn away after the piecing is completed. It is difficult to make a mistake and the results are astonishing.

The plain areas in the blocks are cut using freezer paper patterns. Read more about how to make and use the block patterns and my free-motion quilting designs on page 95.

In this book, I have combined a wide variety of block designs with a large selection of fabric styles. There are fourteen quilt projects in all—something to suit everyone's taste, from the very traditional *Red Licorice* to the contemporary *Sorbet Sunrise*, with lots of other quilts in between. Each project includes details about the quilt construction, fabric choices, and approach to quilting. These "quilter's journals" will help you in making decisions about your own quilts. A final section explains how I created *Joshua Tree*. This pictorial quilt uses New York Beauty blocks in quite a different way. I hope it will inspire you.

I couldn't write a book without including some inspirational photographs. I am a trained black-and-white photographer and have taught myself color photography. I find design ideas everywhere I point my camera lens. The radial images I have captured on film to use for my own study appear throughout the book. I hope they will help you create the most exciting New York Beauty blocks ever.

This page: I love photographing flowers, especially the centers. They display such incredible variety of colors and textures.

Carnival Beauty

et this small, attainable quilt introduce you to the art of New York Beauties. Basic blocks help you master the technical aspects of piecing an arc with points, while two different block sizes in warm and cool colors keep the piecing interesting. The final block layout moves your eye around the quilt, from the top left, across and down, and then back up again. The warm-to-cool color flow follows the same path, enhancing the circular movement of the design. This is a great beginner quilt, both for its technical piecing and the opportunity to play with color movement and transitions. Block sizes: 4" x 4" and 8" x 8". Quilt size: 38" x 42".

otherwise appear too subdued. In the lower right corner, bright turquoise points swing a 180-degree arc, poising the viewer for the return journey across the quilt and back up the left side.

You can take this idea of circulating colors and try it with other palettes, such as yellow to red, green to blue, or pink to purple. The block layout lends itself to numerous possibilities. When you move the color around the quilt, your eye follows, echoing the arcs in the New York Beauties.

Fabric Selection

I had already sketched out the block design for this quilt when I began thinking about the palette. As I looked at the blocks circling around, I realized I could carry out the same idea with color. I had a collection of warm and cool plaids and stripes that had been waiting for the right quilt. Visualizing warm yellows and cool blues was easy for me. My problem was how to intermix the two.

Using the plaids as a theme, I started pulling solid color fabrics to match: yellow, rust, pink, purple, blue, turquoise, lime green. As the palette emerged, it became clear that purples—ranging from red burgundy to deep blue violet—would bridge the gap between warm and cool.

Starting with warm yellows and oranges in the top left block, I moved the warm colors across and down the quilt top, gradually increasing the red burgundy. I let a bit of blue and turquoise infiltrate the warm areas before turning totally cool along the lower edge and up the left side. Splashes of burgundy and orange in the cool area make the transition less abrupt. Lime green practically popped off the surface; I discovered I needed it to brighten up the cooler areas, which would

Quilting

When I sat down to quilt *Carnival Beauty*, I had playful images in mind: balloons, confetti, merry-go-rounds. I quilted one block at a time, making free-form circles and wavy lines and filling in the spaces with simple geometric shapes. Sometimes the quilting was the same on both sides of the block, and other times it varied. Given the playful theme, this was fine with me.

I like the happy accidents that occur in machine quilting. In this quilt, I realized that I was leaving

Carnival Beauty Quilting Designs

the small New York Beauty block points unstitched. I liked the way these small, unstitched points stood out and became more three-dimensional, so I made them all that way.

I found a variegated thread in the quilt colorways to use for quilting. I liked the way the changing thread and plaid colors intermingled. From the theme to the colors, this piece was fun to quilt. I think it is important to enjoy the process as well as the finished product.

Above: A brilliant palette courtesy of a Gloriosa daisy.

Enlarge as desired

Paper-Piecing an Arc

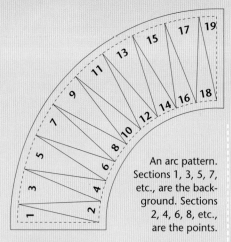

An arc pattern. Sections 1, 3, 5, 7, etc., are the background. Sections 2, 4, 6, 8, etc., are the points.

Use this method to stitch any arc with points. You will need a new paper pattern (see page 95) for each arc you make. You may find it helpful to prefold the point stitching lines before you begin.

1. Set the sewing machine stitch length at 18 to 20 stitches per inch (1.5 setting on a Bernina).

2. Place the two contrasting B strips right sides together, the background fabric on top and the point fabric underneath. Place pattern B on top, marked side up, so that section 1 rests on top of the fabrics and the stitching line is ¼" in from the right edge of the strips. Pin if desired. Stitch on the line, from one curved edge to the other.

3. Turn the work pattern side down. Flip the point fabric over the ¼" seam allowance, and finger-press the seam.

4. Turn the work pattern side up. Using scissors, carefully trim away

the background fabric only even with the edge of the paper pattern.

5. Fold back and crease the paper pattern on the next stitching line (the line between sections 2 and 3). Using scissors or a rotary cutter, trim the point fabric ¼" beyond the folded edge. Trim off the excess point fabric even with the pattern edge. Do not unfold the pattern yet.

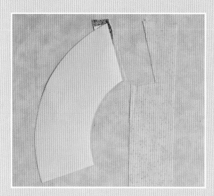

6. Lay the background strip right side up. Place the work on top, pattern side up, and align the raw edges of the background strip and the point fabric. The fabrics will be right sides together.

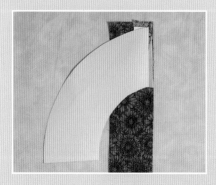

7. Unfold the pattern so the marked side faces up. Stitch on the line, from one curved edge to the other.

8. Turn the work pattern side down. Flip the background fabric over the ¼" seam allowance to reveal the first point. Finger-press the seam.

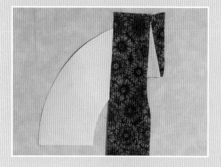

9. Repeat steps 4–8, alternating between the two fabrics, until the entire arc is pieced. Press on the right side. Trim the excess fabric even with the pattern edge. Tear off and discard the paper pattern. Paper piecing will dull your sewing machine needle, so be prepared to change it often.

Once the B arc with points is complete, it can be joined to fabric sections A and C to complete the block. Pieces A and C are cut using freezer paper patterns (see page 95). Here's how to sew the curved seams:

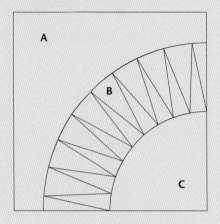

1. Using sharp scissors, make 1/8" clips every 1/2" along the inside curved edge of piece A. Evenly spaced clips are essential for a smooth curved seam.

2. Fold piece A in half to locate the middle of the curved seam, and mark with a pin. In the same way, fold and mark the outside curved edge of pieced arc B.

3. Place A and B right sides together, matching the pins. Pin through both layers at the midpoint, and then remove the marker pins. Line up the straight side edges and pin.

4. With piece A (the concave edge) on top, stitch along the curve 1/4" from the edge for about 1". Stop and realign the raw edges, using a pin to ease the fabric into position. Then resume sewing. The curve is gentle enough that the process should go smoothly. Continue in this way until the entire seam is sewn. Do not press.

5. Repeat step 1 to clip the inside curved edge of B. Repeat step 2 to pin-mark the curved edges of B and C.

6. Repeat steps 3 and 4 to join B and C.

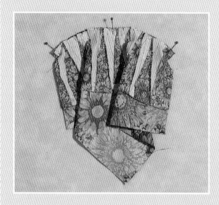

7. On the wrong side, press each seam away from the pieced arc. Press again from the right side. Apply a light coat of spray starch to stabilize the block.

Materials

1¾ yards total assorted cool plaids and stripes (blues, greens, violets), including ½ yard for outer border

⅞ yard total assorted warm plaids and stripes (yellows, reds, olive green, burgundy)

⅝ yard purple (for inner border and piecing)

½ yard burgundy

¼ yard green (for middle border and piecing)

1 fat quarter (18" x 22") each:
  yellow
  orange
  pink/orange print
  violet
  navy blue

Scraps (12" x 12"):
  lavender
  turquoise/navy print
  teal
  turquoise
  blue/green print

¼ yard for binding

1⅜ yards backing

43" x 47" batting

Cutting

Color plays such a vital role in this quilt design, you may want to select and cut the fabrics one block at a time. To base your block colors on the featured quilt, follow the instructions below and refer to the diagram and fabric key on page 14. For each block, first pair up two high-contrast fabrics for the B arc and then choose fabric(s) for A and C to go with them. Follow the same approach when developing your own color palette.

4" BLOCKS (24)

Use the 4" block patterns on page 15, enlarging as indicated. Prepare 24 B paper-piecing patterns. Prepare freezer paper patterns A and C.

Above: A young Gloriosa daisy sprouts fresh yellow-green petals.

For the B arcs, cut 48 strips, each 2¼" x 10", from the assorted fabrics (5 cool plaids/stripes, 4 yellow, 6 orange, 5 pink/orange print, 4 burgundy, 8 purple, 3 lavender, 8 navy blue, 2 turquoise, and 3 green).

Cut 24 A (8 cool plaids/stripes, 8 warm plaids/stripes, 2 pink/orange print, 1 burgundy, 1 purple, 2 navy blue, 1 turquoise/navy print, and 1 turquoise).

Cut 24 C (6 cool plaids/stripes, 9 warm plaids/stripes, 1 orange, 2 pink/orange print, 1 burgundy, 2 turquoise/navy print, 2 blue/green print, and 1 green).

Sort the pieces by block.

8" BLOCKS (8)

Use the 8" block patterns on page 15, enlarging as indicated. Prepare 8 B paper-piecing patterns. Prepare freezer paper patterns A and C.

For the B arcs, cut 16 strips, each 2" x 42", or an equivalent length if using fat quarters and scraps (4 cool plaids/stripes, 3 warm plaids/stripes, 2 yellow, 1 orange, 3 burgundy, 2 purple, and 1 teal).

Cut 8 A (1 cool stripe, 1 warm plaid, 3 warm stripes, 1 burgundy, 1 violet, and 1 navy blue).

Cut 8 C (2 cool plaids/stripes, 1 warm stripe, 1 yellow, 2 pink/orange print, 1 burgundy, and 1 blue/green print).

Sort the pieces by block.

BORDERS

From the purple, cut four 1½" x 42" strips. Cut into two 1½" x 32½" strips for the side inner borders and two 1½" x 30½" strips for the top and bottom inner borders.

From the green, cut four 1" x 42" strips. Cut into two 1" x 34½" strips for the side middle borders and two 1" x 31½" strips for the top and bottom middle borders.

From a cool plaid, cut four 4" x 42" strips. Cut into two 4" x 35½" strips for the side outer borders and two 4" x 38½" strips for the top and bottom outer borders.

Assembly

1. Refer to Paper-Piecing an Arc (page 10) and Joining Curved Sections (page 11). For each block, piece arc B and then join it to pieces A and C. Make twenty-four 4" blocks and eight 8" blocks.

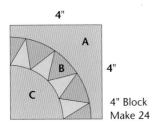

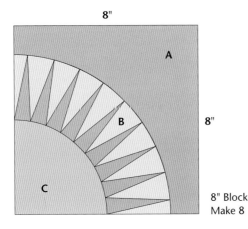

4" Block
Make 24

8" Block
Make 8

2. Lay out the blocks as shown in the quilt diagram (page 14). Stitch the 4" blocks together in pairs (blocks 1 and 4, 2 and 5, 3 and 6, etc.) to make twelve 4" x 8" units. Press. Join the

4" x 8" units and the 8" blocks together in rows. Press. Join the rows. Press.

3. Add the side inner borders to the quilt. Press. Add the top and bottom inner borders. Press. Add the middle and outer borders in the same sequence, pressing after each addition.

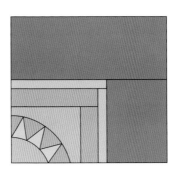

Border Corner Detail

4. Layer and finish the quilt.

Carnival Beauty Quilting Design
Enlarge as desired

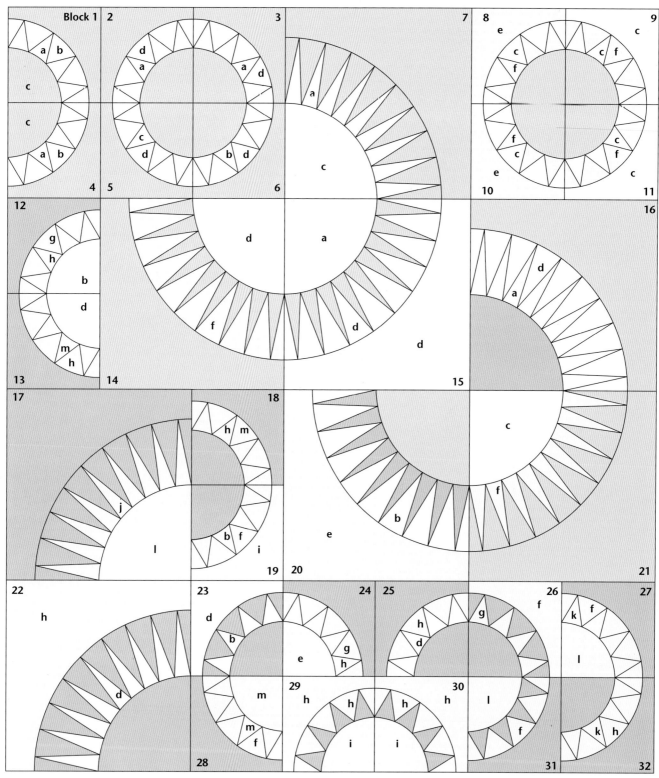

QUILT DIAGRAM

Fabric Key

| | warm plaid/stripe |
| | cool plaid/stripe |

a   yellow
b   orange
c   pink/orange print

d   burgundy
e   violet
f   purple
g   lavender
h   navy blue

i   turquoise/navy print
j   teal
k   turquoise
l   blue/green print
m   green

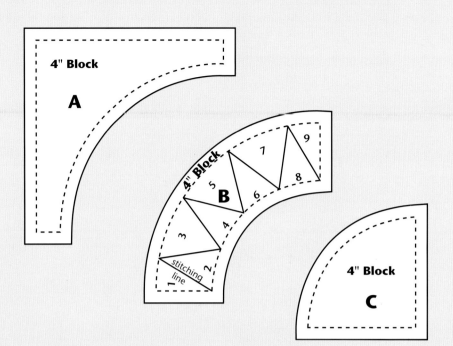

4" Block

A

4" Block

B

5
7
9
3
6
8
4
2
stitching line
1

4" Block

C

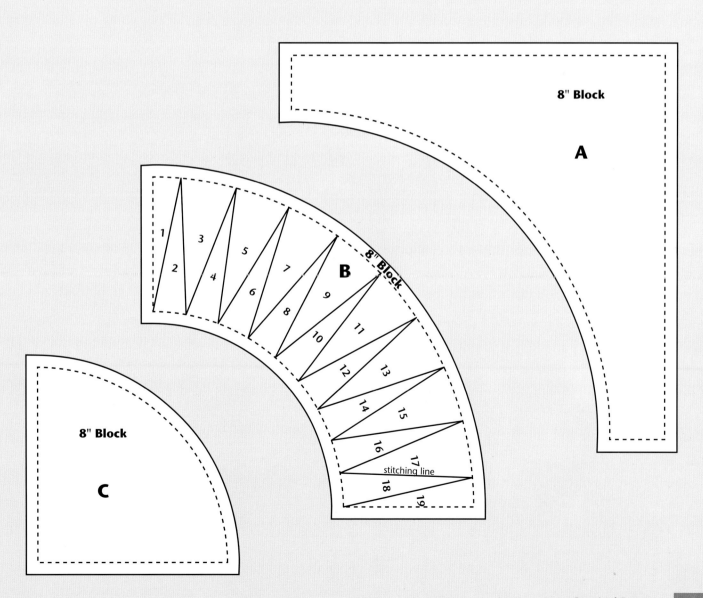

8" Block

A

8" Block

B

1
2
3
4
5
6
7
8
9
10
11
12
13
14
15
16
17
18
19
stitching line

8" Block

C

Carnival Beauty Quilting Designs
Enlarge as desired

Radiant New York Beauties

Vintage Beauty

Vintage-style textiles are loaded with historical interest, especially when combined in a scrappy quilt. In this quilt, two different eight-inch blocks add up to four large circles. The multiple arcs and points create a lot of visual rotation, while four smaller blocks anchor the quilt's outside corners. The plain setting, traditional sashing, and appliquéd vine-and-leaf border carry out the vintage look. Block sizes: 4" x 4" and 8" x 8". Quilt size: 42" x 42".

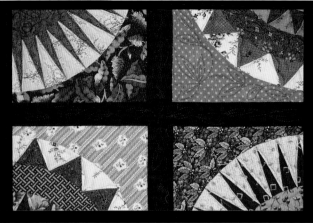

Fabric Selection

In scrap quilts, it is especially important to plan for contrast between light, medium, and dark fabrics. Without contrast, all those carefully pieced arcs won't show up.

I started by choosing multicolor prints for the large A sections of the blocks. The A section forms two edges of the block and is fairly prominent. The fabrics used here helped set the mood of the quilt. Once they were chosen, I looked for "blenders." Blenders are prints with subtle designs and very low contrast. From a distance, they read as slightly textured or solid. It's good to include some strong darks so that when blenders are placed side by side, the points show up. Finally, I looked over my selections to identify a few interesting accent colors. One of the prints had some nice blue-green, and I also liked the bubble gum pink. They make the palette sparkle.

When I am working in a palette of prints, I begin by laying out the theme fabric I have chosen for section A. Next I look for a combination of two fabrics for the arc B

points and background. I audition both of these fabrics together and next to the theme fabric. Finally, I audition multicolor fabrics and accent fabrics for C, or the base of the block. Once I've made my selections, I reevaluate them to make sure that I have a variety of fabrics and that I haven't overmatched them. The first block may not appear too interesting, but once you have several made, the colors will begin to dance

Vintage Beauty Quilting Designs

around and the palette will start appearing more energetic. You always need to make a few blocks before you see the palette working.

The second block design in *Vintage Beauty* contains multiple pieced arcs. Here is an opportunity to mix up the fabrics even more and repeat the color combinations used previously with different shapes. Always lay out all of the fabrics when making your choices. Make sure the fabrics work in the new block as well as with the blocks you already have made.

Quilting

In keeping with the traditional style of *Vintage Beauty*, the points are quilted on each side of the seam. Even if your sewing is not perfectly straight, the overall look is still very effective. The remainder of the blocks are filled in with leaf shapes that mimic the appliqués in the border. This creates a theme for the quilt and adds repetition to the design.

Above: I love the interior of this bowl. The design is so simple, yet it can inspire in so many ways. The concentric designs give me color ideas for multiple pieced arcs. There are quilting designs here too, waiting to be discovered.

Enlarge as desired

Needleturn Appliqué

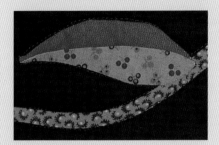

Needleturn appliqué is an easy method of hand appliqué for beginners to learn.

1. Trace and cut out the freezer paper template. Place the template shiny side down on the right side of the fabric. Press with a warm, dry iron for a few seconds, just until it adheres.

2. Cut out the appliqué a scant ¼" beyond the edge of the freezer paper template all around. Remove the template or leave it in place—whichever will be more comfortable for you as you appliqué.

3. Turn under the outside edge of the appliqué a scant ¼", or just beyond the edge of the freezer paper template, if it is still attached. Finger-press to give the edge a little memory.

4. Position the appliqué on the background fabric, right sides up. Pin from the wrong side so that the appliqué thread will not get caught on the pin point.

5. Thread a #10 milliners needle with an 18" length of thread that matches the appliqué. Take a few short stitches on the wrong side of the background fabric in a concealed location to anchor the thread. Plan to start your stitching along a fairly smooth edge of the appliqué, not at a point or a corner.

6. Bring the needle up from the wrong side and catch one or two threads along the folded edge of the appliqué. Reinsert the needle into the background fabric at almost the same spot and pull through to make a tiny stitch. Carry the thread along the back for approximately ⅛" before bringing it up again. Continue making tiny stitches along the edge of the appliqué. Use the needle to turn under the edge ½" to 1" ahead of where you are currently stitching.

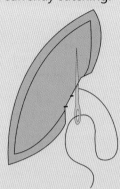

7. To make a sharp point, stitch right up to the point of the fold line. Take the tip of the needle and pull the seam allowance around and under. Continue stitching.

Free-Motion Quilting

To me, free-motion quilting is the icing on the cake. It lets you add those final design lines that help say what your quilt is about. I think about the quilting in the very beginning stages of the quilt design. I may refine my ideas along the way, but the quilting is always an integral part of the overall design.

1. Set up your machine. Attach a clear darning/embroidery foot so that you can see the stitching as it progresses on the surface of the quilt.

2. Drop the feed dogs. With the feed dogs no longer touching the underside of the fabric, you'll be able to move your quilt randomly through the machine—the *free-motion* part of the quilting.

3. Prepare a 20"-square quilt sandwich (fabric, batting, fabric) for practice. Always begin on a practice piece to allow yourself time to get into the rhythm of the stitch length and speed.

4. Begin stitching. Keep a steady, generous amount of pressure on the foot pedal as you maneuver your quilt through the machine. Aim for a stitch length that is neither too close together nor too far apart, about the length of a piecing stitch. Once you learn how to coordinate the movement of the quilt with the speed of the needle, you'll develop your own rhythm. Give yourself five or ten minutes to get a rhythm going before switching over to the quilt. Do this warm-up session each time you sit down to sew.

The design possibilities with free-motion quilting are endless. Keep in mind that quilting lines can go over piecing lines and that a pieced area can be over-layed with a larger quilting design. There are many examples of continuous line designs throughout the book for you to try. Successful free-motion quilting is a combination of creativity, patience, and practice.

- If you don't feel quite sure of a design, make a tracing and lay it over the quilt to audition it. Tracing also helps you memorize the design and prepares you to stitch it freehand. For more on tracing a quilting design, see page 95.

- To mark a free-motion quilting design directly on the fabric, use a transfer pencil, chalk pencil, or washable marker (pretest it first to make sure it will really wash out).

- Once you get into the groove of quilting, you may find that you get ideas of what you would like to quilt and that you don't have to mark the quilt at all. Try tracing organic shapes from photos, magazines, and pictures, and keep a file of ideas. Sketch simple designs and then refine them so that they can be sewn as a single continous line. The fabrics in your quilt can also suggest lines and shapes to repeat.

Materials

12 fat quarters (18" x 22") in assorted brown, cream, pink, and green prints, including a brown theme print

⅛ yard each twelve coordinating prints, plaids, and textured solids

1⅛ yards dark brown (includes ¼ yard for binding)

¼ yard green print (for vine)

1⅜ yards backing

46" x 46" batting

#10 milliners needle

Cutting

Select and cut the fabrics one block at a time. Choose the fabric for A first. Then pair up two high-contrast fabrics for each pieced arc. Choose fabrics for the adjacent solid area(s) last.

8" BLOCKS (8)

Use the 8" block patterns on page 15, enlarging as indicated. Prepare 8 B paper-piecing patterns. Prepare freezer paper patterns A and C.

From the fat quarters, cut 8 A (at least two from the theme print).

From the assorted fabrics, cut 16 strips, each 3½" x 42", or an equivalent length if using fat quarters, for B.

From the assorted fabrics, cut 8 C.

Sort the pieces by block.

8" VARIATION BLOCKS (8)

Use the 8" variation block patterns on page 24, enlarging as indicated. Prepare 8 B and 8 D paper-piecing patterns. Prepare freezer paper patterns A, C, and E.

From the fat quarters, cut 8 A.

From the assorted fabrics, cut 16 strips, each 3¼" x 12", for B, and 16 strips, each 2¼" x 10", for D.

From the assorted fabrics, cut 8 C and 8 E.

Sort the pieces by block.

4" BLOCKS (4)

Use the 4" block patterns on page 15, enlarging as indicated. Prepare 4 B paper-piecing patterns. Prepare freezer paper patterns A and C.

From the dark brown, cut 4 A and one 2¼" x 42" strip for B.

From the assorted prints, cut four 2¼" x 10" strips for B (or use scraps from other pieced blocks).

From the brown theme print, cut 4 C.

Sort the pieces by block.

SASHING & BORDER

Use the leaf appliqué patterns on page 24 to prepare freezer paper templates A, B, C, and D.

Refer to Needleturn Appliqué (page 20). From the assorted block scraps, cut 4 A, 4 B, 4 C, and 4 D leaf appliqués, or 16 pieces total.

From the green print, cut several 1⅜"-wide strips on the bias (use the 45° mark on your cutting ruler). Piece together to make one 1⅜" x 26" strip and one 1⅜" x 22" strip for the vine appliqués.

From the dark brown, cut two 2" x 42" strips. Cut into two 2" x 16½" strips for the horizontal sashing and one 2" x 34" strip for the vertical sashing. Cut four 4½" x 42" strips. Cut into four 4½" x 34" strips for the border.

Assembly

1. Refer to Paper-Piecing an Arc (page 10) and Joining Curved Sections (page 11). For each 8" block, piece arc B and then join it to pieces A and C. Make eight blocks total.

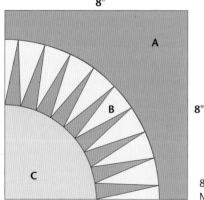

8"

8"

8" Block
Make 8

2. For each 8" variation block, piece arcs B and D and join them to pieces A, C, and E. Make eight blocks total.

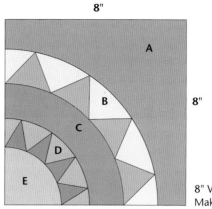

8"

8"

8" Variation Block
Make 8

3. For each 4" block, paper-piece a B arc using dark brown for the background. Join arc B and pieces A and C. Make four blocks total.

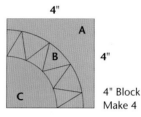

4"

4"

4" Block
Make 4

4. Lay out all the 8" blocks to form four radiating circles, as shown in the quilt photograph (page 17) and quilt diagram. Stitch the blocks together in groups of four, pressing as you go. Join together in two columns, inserting horizontal sashing strips in between. Press. Join the columns, inserting a vertical sashing strip in between. Press.

5. Arrange the border strips around the quilt top. Position a 4" block at each outside corner so that the arc points face out. Join the side borders to the quilt top. Press. Stitch the 4" blocks to the top and bottom borders. Press. Join to the quilt top. Press.

6. Fold each green bias strip in half lengthwise, right side out. Fold in one end ¼" and press. Starting at the lower right corner of the quilt top, place the longer strip on the bottom border and the shorter strip on the right side border. Pin the folded end even with the corner block seam. Continue pinning along the length of each strip, curving it to form a vinelike shape. Machine-stitch a scant ¼" from the long raw edges through all layers. Press the folded edge over the seam allowance and slipstitch in place.

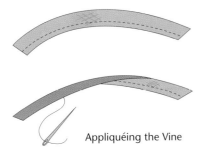

Appliquéing the Vine

7. Stitch the leaf pieces together in AB and CD pairs. If you use a scant ¼" seam allowance, you'll find that these gently curved seams ease together nicely without clipping. Press. Refer to Needleturn Appliqué (page 20). Position four leaves along each vine and appliqué in place.

8. Layer and quilt as desired.

QUILT DIAGRAM

Block Key

■ 8" block

■ 8" variation block

■ 4" block

Enlarge all patterns 200%. For additional information on making paper-piecing and freezer paper patterns, see page 95.

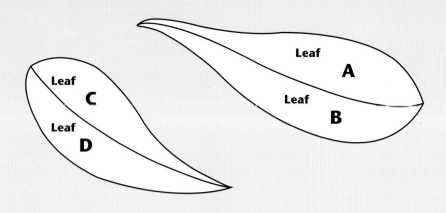

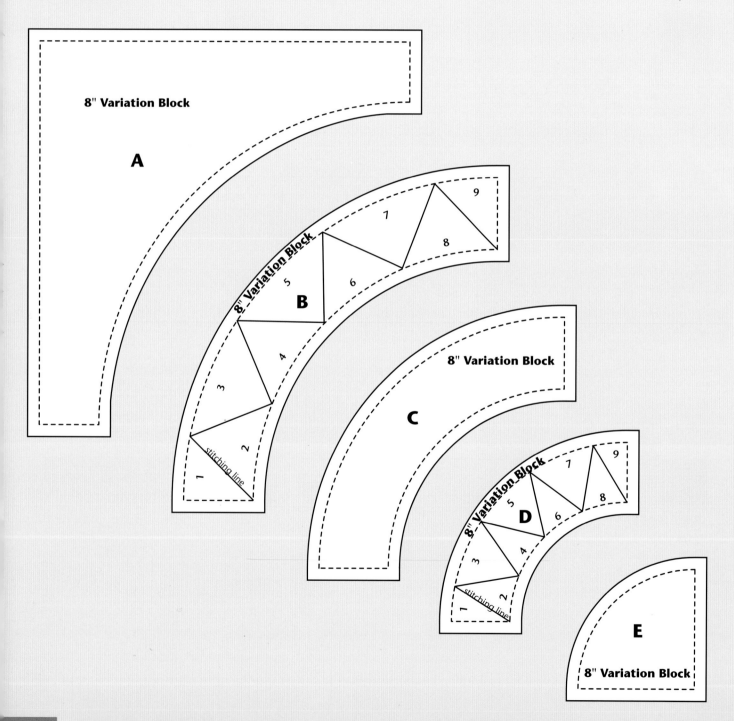

Posy Pots

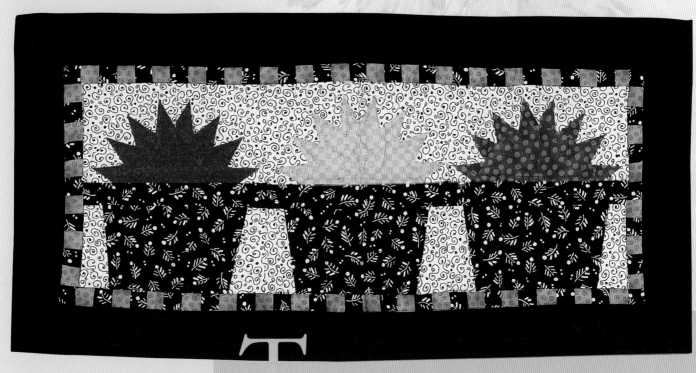

T wo four-inch New York Beauty blocks placed side by side make perfect flowers for a spring wall hanging. I designed the containers to look like classic clay pot shapes. A checked border adds a whimsical touch. Block size: 4" x 4" and 5" x 8". Quilt size: 13½" x 28½".

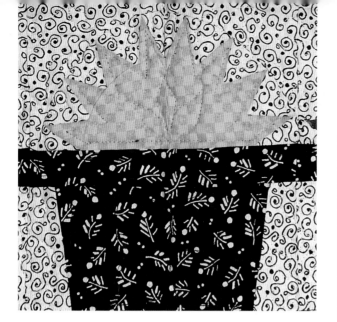

Fabric Selection

When these black-and-white prints first came out, I just had to find a way to use them. I liked their stylized character and the petite size of the motifs. I decided a small wall hanging would offer the right scale for viewing them.

Bright clear primary colors seemed a natural coupled with the black and white backgrounds. Working with this palette, I came up with the idea of flowers in individual pots. The four-inch New York Beauty block is the same one used in *Carnival Beauty* and *Vintage Beauty*. This time, only two fabrics are used for each block to create a flower shape. I drafted several flowerpots until I got the right shape and proportions to go with the flowers.

What are flowers without a bit of garden greenery? Since I didn't have leaves in the design, I improvised by surrounding my blooms with a green-and-black-checked border. You could easily make rows and rows of these flowerpot blocks if you wanted a larger quilt.

Quilting

Each flower point is outline-quilted to emphasize its shape. Softer, more rounded petal designs are quilted inside each flower head. The curlicues in the white background print inspired the free-motion quilting that fills this area. A continuous-line swirl is quilted in the black border all around.

Materials

½ yard black-on-white print

½ yard white-on-black print

⅛ yard each red, yellow, blue, and green textured solids

⅜ yard black (includes ¼ yard for binding)

½ yard backing

18" x 33" batting

Cutting

4" BLOCKS (6)

Use the 4" block patterns on page 15, enlarging as indicated. Prepare 6 B paper-piecing patterns. Prepare freezer paper patterns A and C.

From the black-on-white print, cut 4 A and four 2¼" x 10" strips for B.

From the red, the yellow, and the blue, cut two 2¼" x 10" strips each for B and 2 C each.

Sort the pieces by block.

FLOWERPOT BLOCKS (3)

Use the patterns on page 28 to prepare freezer paper patterns D, E, and Er.

From the white-on-black print, cut 3 D and three 1½" x 8½" strips (F).

From the black-on-white print, cut 3 E and 3 Er.

BORDERS

From the green and the white-on-black print, cut two 1¼" x 42" strips each for the inner border.

From the black solid, cut two 2" x 42" strips. Cut each strip into one 2" x 11" strip for the side outer border and one 2" x 28½" strip for the top/bottom outer border. Set aside the remaining black for the binding.

Assembly

1. Refer to Paper-Piecing an Arc (page 10) and Joining Curved Sections (page 11). Paper-piece 6 B arcs with red, yellow, or blue points and black-on-white print backgrounds. Join arc B

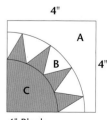

4" Block
Make 6 assorted

and pieces A and C, matching the B and C colors, to make six blocks total.

2. Stitch the 4" blocks together in pairs, matching the colors. Press. Stitch E and Er to each D. Press. Lay out the pieced units and strip F as shown. Stitch together in rows. Press.

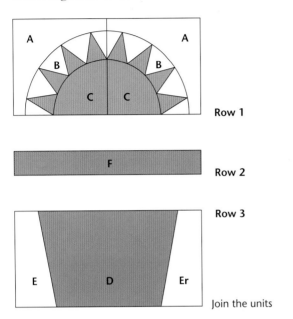

Row 1

Row 2

Row 3

Join the units

3. Lay out the three flowerpot units side by side, as shown in the quilt photograph (page 25) and quilt

diagram. Stitch together to make the center panel of the wall hanging. Press. Use a rotary cutter and ruler to trim the center panel to 8¾" x 23¾", so that the inner checked border will fit exactly. (If you prefer, trim the units before you join them to achieve the same dimensions.)

4. Stitch the green and white-on-black strips together along the long edges, alternating the colors. Press. Cut the strip set into 1¼" segments.

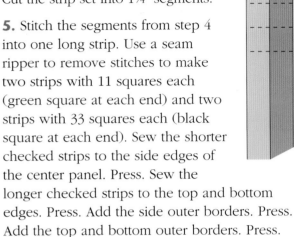

1¼"

5. Stitch the segments from step 4 into one long strip. Use a seam ripper to remove stitches to make two strips with 11 squares each (green square at each end) and two strips with 33 squares each (black square at each end). Sew the shorter checked strips to the side edges of the center panel. Press. Sew the longer checked strips to the top and bottom edges. Press. Add the side outer borders. Press. Add the top and bottom outer borders. Press.

6. Layer and quilt as desired.

QUILT DIAGRAM

Block Key

[ ] 4" block

[ ] Flowerpot block

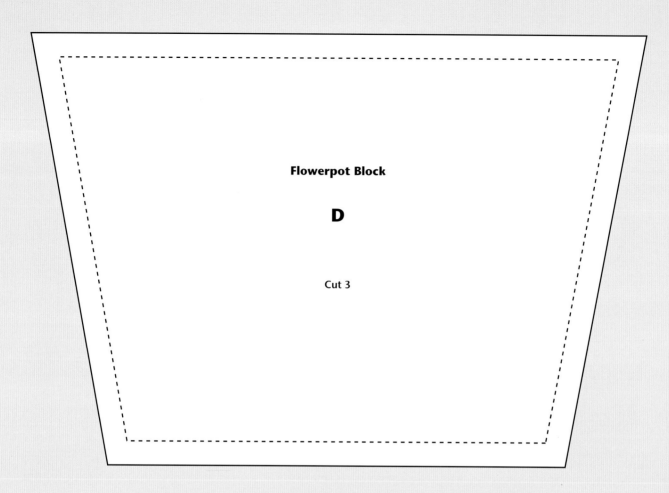

Flowerpot Block

D

Cut 3

Photocopy at 100%. For additional information on making paper-piecing and freezer paper patterns, see page 95.

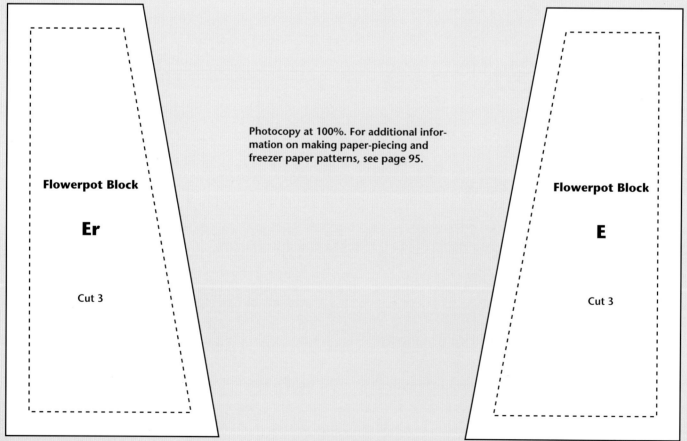

Flowerpot Block

Er

Cut 3

Flowerpot Block

E

Cut 3

Red Licorice

Red Licorice is an example of how New York Beauty blocks are traditionally pieced and arranged. To get design ideas for this quilt, I looked at old family-owned quilts and at books featuring New York Beauty quilts. I was attracted to two-color quilts, particularly those using a red-and-white palette. The pieced border echoes and intensifies the arc points in the blocks. Block size: 10" x 10". Quilt size: 48" x 48".

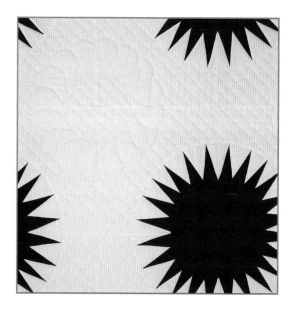

hatched in the center. She stitched in-the-ditch around the points of the New York Beauty blocks and created a small feather medallion for the red centers to echo the larger ones. The border was treated the same way: points stitched in-the-ditch with small medallions at the corners. The quilting is as straightforward and uncomplicated as the palette in this striking quilt.

Red Licorice Quilting Design (sized for red circles)

Fabric Selection

The two-color palette in *Red Licorice* makes the geometric shapes especially sharp and crisp. I chose white solid and a red fabric with tiny black polka dots. The red print has a traditional look and reads as a solid, making it a perfect choice for this New York Beauty revival. In many of the older two-color quilts I studied, the red palette was actually assembled from a variety of scraps, another option to try if you are a fabric collector.

In the older quilts, the blocks were joined by sashing, but I didn't like the way sashing chopped up the arrangement. By dropping the sashing and enlarging the blocks to ten inches, I was able to come up with the white background space I envisioned for a traditional quilting design. This quilt could be done in a variety of colors and textures. Instead of white, you might use shirting fabrics in solids or subtle stripes.

Quilting

I sent this quilt out to Katrina Beverage, a friend who does beautiful traditional quilting by machine. I find that my quilting style is a little too contemporary, and I wanted the quilt to have an old-fashioned look and feel. Katrina did a beautiful job, filling each of the four large white areas with a feathered medallion that is cross-

Materials

3¼ yards white

2¼ yards red (includes ¼ yard for binding)

1½ yards backing

52" x 52" batting

Cutting

10" BLOCKS (16)

Use the 10" block patterns on page 33, enlarging as indicated. Prepare 16 B paper-piecing patterns. Prepare freezer paper patterns A and C.

From the white, cut 16 A and six 3" x 42" strips for B.

From the red, cut six 2" x 42" strips for B and 16 C.

BORDER

Use the D border unit pattern on page 33, enlarging as indicated. Prepare 16 D paper-piecing patterns.

From the white and the red, cut sixteen 2" x 42" strips each for D.

From the red, cut one 4½" x 42" strip. Cut into four 4½" squares (E).

Assembly

1. Refer to Paper-Piecing an Arc (page 10) and Joining Curved Sections (page 11). Paper-piece 16 B arcs with red points and white backgrounds. Join arc B and pieces A and C to make 16 blocks total.

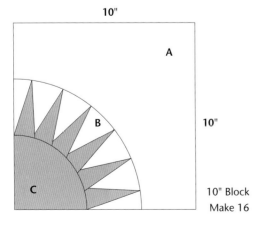

10"

A

B

C

10"

10" Block
Make 16

2. Paper-piece 16 D border units, using red for the points and white for the backgrounds.

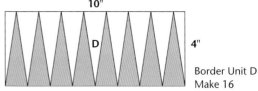

10"

D

4"

Border Unit D
Make 16

3. Lay out the blocks in four rows of four blocks each, as shown in the quilt photograph (page 29) and quilt diagram (page 32). Sew the blocks together in rows. Press. Join the rows. Press.

4. Stitch the D border units together in four groups of four, making sure all the red points face the same direction. Press. Arrange the borders around the quilt top so the red falls toward the outside edge. Sew the side borders to the quilt top. Press. Stitch the 4½" corner squares to the top and bottom borders. Press. Join to the quilt top. Press.

5. Layer and quilt as desired.

Below: The colors in this leaf would translate beautifully into a quilt.

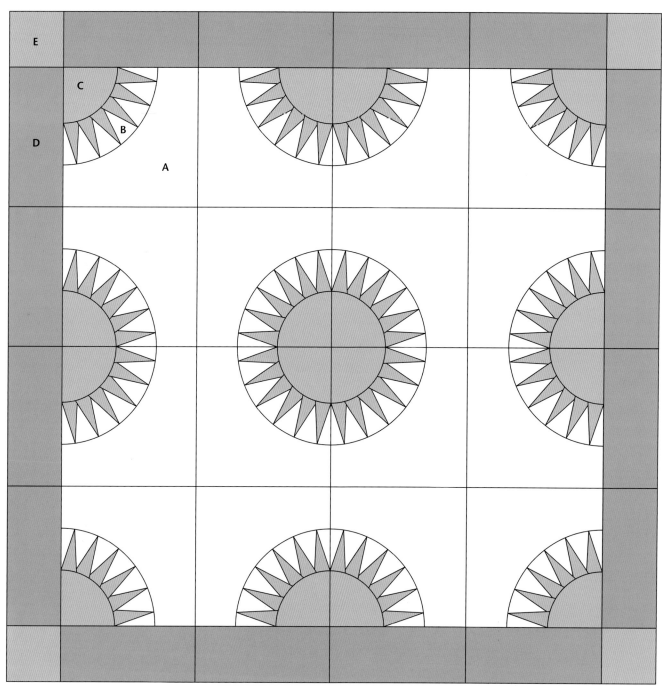

QUILT DIAGRAM

Enlarge all patterns 200%.
For additional information on
making paper-piecing and
freezer paper patterns, see
page 95.

10" Block

A

10" Block

stitching line

1

2

3

4

5

6

7

8

9

10

11

12

13

B

10" Block

10" Block

C

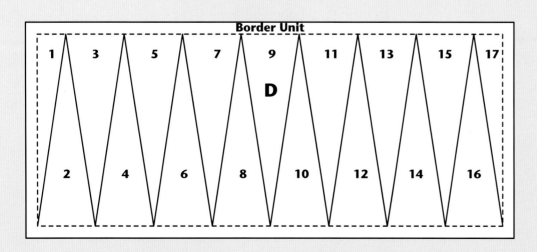

Border Unit

1 3 5 7 9 11 13 15 17

D

2 4 6 8 10 12 14 16

Yee-hah!

just loved this cowgirl theme print when it first came into the store. The girls were sassy and a little risqué. I couldn't wait to figure out how to feature them in a quilt. *Yee-hah!* uses the same New York Beauty block and layout as *Red Licorice*, but the colors, textures, and sashing strips take it in a totally different direction. Around the outside edge, mitered corners show off a wood-grain border and enhance the framing effect. The mini lesson on page 37 explains how it's done. Block size: 10" x 10". Quilt size: 54" x 54".

Fabric Selection

A theme print works in a New York Beauty quilt if you know how to use it. Motifs the size of these cowgirls would lose their charm if cut up for arcs and points, but over a larger background area, they're perfect. I had to fussy-cut the fabric to get all the girls facing the same way. Fussy-cutting does take more thought and more fabric, but the result is worth it.

I based my other fabrics on the cowgirl theme print. Bandana prints in red and blue pick up on the western theme. They appear in the arc points and centers. They were too busy and complex to serve as backgrounds too, so I found a deep red plaid and denim blue solid to use instead.

When I got all of the blocks sewn and up on the wall, the quilt just died. I wasn't exactly sure what to do next. I started playing around with sashing ideas, using red and blue plaids. I didn't want to break up the circle in the center of the quilt, so I ran the strips around it, offsetting the red and the blue to create the woven effect. The sashing inspired the red and blue inner borders, but the outer border had me stumped. When I took another look at the cowgirls, sitting on those woody split rail fences, I had my answer.

Quilting

Patricia Raymond did the machine quilting in *Yee-hah!* The fabrics provided several ideas for the quilting motifs we chose. I didn't want to outline the cowgirls, but a cactus was a design that could easily be repeated with free-motion quilting. The bandana prints gave me paisleys. The outer border offered plenty of irregular lines for stitching and enhancing the rugged wood-grain print. When you take the time to look at your fabric and simplify the design, you can find plenty of quilting ideas.

Below: This photo is actually of a gate, but viewed close-up, the design radiates like a New York beauty.

The points in this block are narrow, so Patricia simply outlined them rather than trying to stitch inside. It's important to outline a block or stitch in-the-ditch even if you don't do any further quilting. Outlining secures the quilt sandwich and makes the quilt surface even.

Yee-hah! Quilting Designs
Enlarge as desired

Mitered corners give border strips a neat diagonal seam at the corners. Cut the border strips as the project directs, or about 5" longer than the finished quilt edge. If there are multiple borders, sew the strips together and treat them as one unit to make the miter.

Above: Mitering enhances the framing effect of a striped border.

1. Fold a border strip in half crosswise to locate the midpoint of the long inner edge. Mark the midpoint with a pin. In the same way, mark the midpoint of the corresponding edge of the quilt top.

2. Place the border strip on the quilt, right sides together and pins matching. Pin at the middle and at the corners, allowing the excess border to extend evenly at each end. Stitch together, starting and stopping ¼" from the edge at the corners of the quilt. Press toward the border.

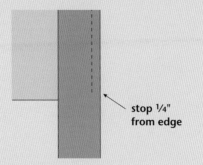

stop ¼" from edge

3. Repeat steps 1 and 2 to join the adjacent border.

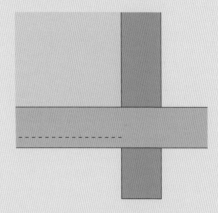

4. Lay the quilt right side up on the ironing board. Let one border overlap the other border. Fold the top border back on itself at a 45° angle.

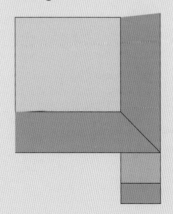

5. Use a triangle or a rotary cutting grid ruler to check the angle, and then press the fold.

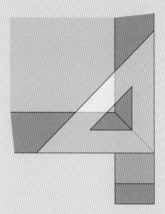

6. Fold the quilt, right side in, on the diagonal, and pin the two border strips together. Beginning at the inside corner of the quilt, stitch on the fold line to the outer edge. Trim off the excess fabric, for a ¼" seam allowance. Press the seam open. Repeat steps 3–6 until all four corners are mitered.

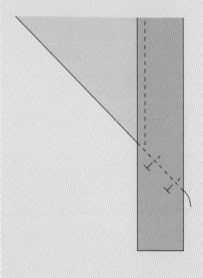

Materials

1¼ yards cowgirl theme print (be sure to add extra for fussy-cutting)

1 yard wood-grain print (includes ¼ yard for binding)

½ yard red bandana print

½ yard blue bandana print

½ yard deep red plaid

½ yard denim blue

⅓ yard red plaid

⅓ yard blue plaid

3¼ yards backing

58" x 58" batting

Cutting

10" BLOCKS (16)

Use the 10" block patterns on page 33, enlarging as indicated. Prepare 16 B paper-piecing patterns. Prepare freezer paper patterns A and C.

From the theme print, cut 16 A. Refer to the block orientation in the quilt photograph (page 34) to fussy-cut these pieces. You will need to orient the pattern on the fabric four different ways, cutting four pieces each time.

From the deep red plaid and the denim blue, cut five 3" x 42" strips each for the outer points of B, or ten total.

From the red and the blue bandana prints, cut five 2" x 42" strips each for the inner points of B, or ten total. Also cut 8 C from each, or 16 total.

SASHING

From the red plaid, cut two 1½" x 42" strips. Cut into four 1½" x 10½" strips and two 1½" x 20½" strips for the vertical sashing. Also cut two 1½" squares.

From the blue plaid, cut two 1½" x 42" strips. Cut into four 1½" x 10½" strips and two 1½" x 20½" strips for the horizontal sashing. Also cut two 1½" squares.

BORDER

From the red plaid, cut three 2½" x 42" strips. Sew into one long strip. Cut into two 2½" x 42½" strips for the side inner borders. (Note: If your fabric width allows, cut the strips without piecing.)

From the blue plaid, cut three 2½" x 42" strips. Sew into one long strip. Cut into two 2½" x 46½" strips for the top and bottom inner borders.

From the wood-grain fabric, cut six 4½" x 42" strips. Sew into one long strip. Cut into four 4½" x 54½" strips for the outer borders.

Assembly

1. Refer to Paper-Piecing an Arc (page 10). Paper-piece 8 B arcs with blue bandana print points and deep red plaid backgrounds. Paper-piece 8 B arcs with red bandana print points and denim blue backgrounds.

2. Refer to Joining Curved Sections (page 11). Join the B arcs and pieces A and C. For each block, match C to the B point fabric. If you fussy-cut the A pieces, be sure to match them to the B's as planned. Make 16 blocks total.

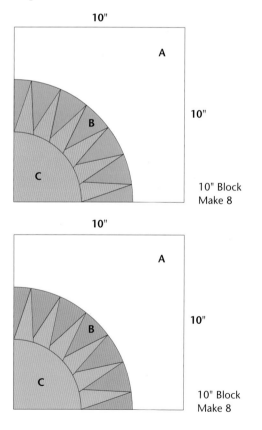

10"

A

B

C

10"

10"

10" Block Make 8

10"

A

B

C

10"

10" Block Make 8

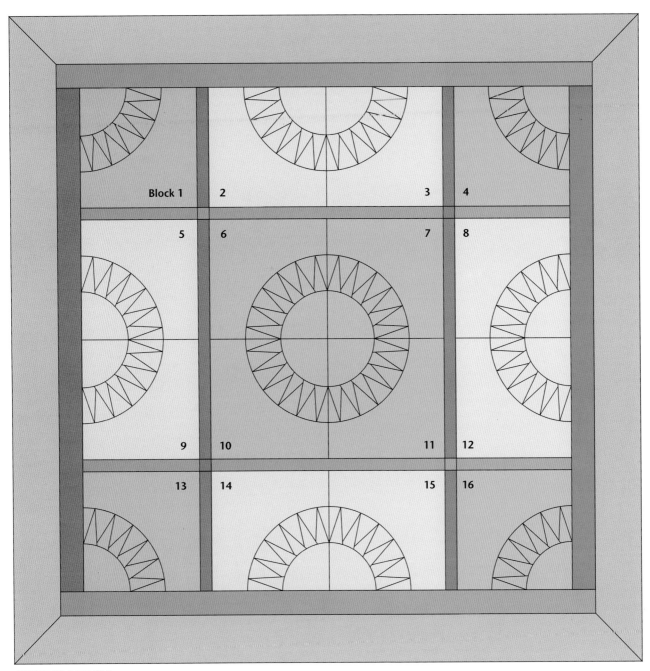

QUILT DIAGRAM

3. Lay out the blocks in four rows of four blocks each, as shown in the quilt photograph (page 34) and quilt diagram. Stitch the blocks together in pairs to make six semicircle units (blocks 2 and 3, 6 and 7, etc.) Press. Join two semicircle units to complete the circle at the center of the quilt top. Press.

4. Stitch the blocks and units together in three rows, inserting vertical sashing strips in between.

Press. Stitch the horizontal sashing strips and sashing squares together. Press. Join the rows and horizontal sashing strips. Press.

5. Sew the side inner borders to the quilt top. Press. Add the top and bottom inner borders. Press. Refer to Making Mitered Corners (page 37) to attach and complete the wood-grain borders.

6. Layer and quilt as desired.

Radiant Beauty

*R*adiant Beauty introduces an irregular New York Beauty block. The points are varied in size and overlap at random, creating playful movement. To make the piecing match at each side, the block is flipped over and joined to its mirror image. This is the first irregular block I drafted, and I found the process unexpectedly gratifying. (Learn more about my drafting and sewing methods in the mini lessons on pages 42 and 54–55.) The other fun part of this quilt is the extra-wide border—a full eight strips deep—with mitered corners. The added color bands frame the quilt and help contain the exuberant arcs that seem to spin within. Block size: 11" x 11". Quilt size: 70" x 70".

Fabric Selection

At The Stitchin' Post, we do an employee quilt challenge every year. In 2000, our challenge was to create a quilt using a fabric collection that I designed called "Through the Garden Gate." My favorite fabric in the collection shows a frog on a leaf. I was determined to use it but knew the frogs were too big and the print far too busy to read as New York Beauty points. Instead, I decided to try the frog fabric as the background for my blocks. A few subtle batiks and hand-dyed fabrics in similar colors became my choice for the background points.

I started out by making four blocks with yellow points, butting them up to create a sunlike shape in the center of the quilt. Rather than making the rest of the blocks a rainbow of colors, I chose one color scheme for all of them and just varied the fabrics. The points were always purple and they radiated out from a red or pink arc, a green arc, and finally a red print at the center. This approach let me use multiple fabrics while keeping the overall palette consistent.

Once I had these sixteen blocks done, I was a little stumped. More blocks would be distracting, but a plain wide border seemed boring and uninspiring. I started playing around with multiple borders in different widths and found this avenue very appealing. Since the quilt already had a lot of green, I didn't put any green in the border. Instead, I pulled in some of the warmer colors in the quilt. Mitering the corners was the final touch to create dimension within the quilt. The narrow black binding is one of my favorite finishes.

Quilting

For this quilt, I let the fabric patterns and piecing seam lines influence my quilting direction. I quilted points in the centers of the New York Beauty blocks and wavy lines in the pieced points. I laid out the quilt and drew mini New York Beauty half-blocks at random in the border and quilted them with purple thread. For the rest of the background and border, I borrowed the leaf outline from the frog fabric, quilting in a continuous line and adding swirly tendrils. This leaf stitching filled in nicely without taking away from the designs in the fabric. I always strive to quilt in a complementary way, to bring the quilt to a satisfying conclusion, but without rushing or hurrying the process.

Paper-Piecing Irregular Points

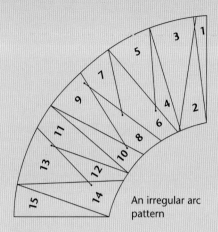

An irregular arc pattern

On a paper-piecing pattern for an irregular arc, the stitching lines do not always extend to the bottom or top edge. The idea is to allow the points to overlap and intersect without excess fabric buildup. Here's how to sew the arc:

Above: Viewing the top of a plant as well as the underside can give you a new perspective on its shape and design.

1. Place the two contrasting B strips right sides together, with the background fabric on top and the point fabric underneath, just as you would for a symmetrical arc (see Paper-Piecing an Arc on page 10). Place pattern B on top, marked side up, so that section 1 rests on top of the fabrics and the stitching line between sections 1 and 2 falls ¼" from the edge of the strips. Pin if desired.

2. Stitch on the line exactly as it is marked on the pattern. If the stitching line stops just beyond the intersection of two lines, start or end your stitching at that point too.

3. Trim *the background fabric only* even with the edge of the paper pattern. Turn the work over, flip back the point fabric, and finger-press the seam, just as you would for a symmetrical arc.

4. Turn the work pattern side up. Fold back and crease the paper pattern on the stitching line that borders section 3. Let the paper tear a bit, if necessary, to accommodate the two or three stitches that cross over the stitching line.

5. Using scissors or a rotary cutter, trim the point fabric ¼" beyond the folded edge. Unfold the pattern and trim off the excess point fabric even with the pattern edge.

6. Refold the pattern on the crease. Lay the background strip right side up. Place the work on

top, pattern side up, and align the raw edges of the point fabric and the background strip. Unfold the pattern, marked side up. Stitch on the line. Some stitching lines extend across the width of the arc and others are shorter. Follow the paper pattern.

7. Turn the work pattern side down. Flip the background fabric over the ¼" seam allowance to reveal the first point. Finger-press the seam.

8. Repeat steps 4–7, alternating between the two fabrics and following the numbered order on the pattern, until the entire arc is pieced. Press on the right side. Trim the excess fabric even with the pattern edge. Tear off and discard the paper pattern.

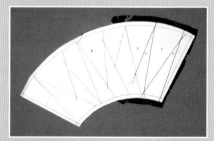

Two points are stitched

A view of the right side

Materials

Blocks:

1½ yards green frog print

1¼ yards muted green

⅔ yard green/brown print

⅝ yard each two different purples

½ yard yellow

Scraps (12" x 12"):
    four assorted red/pink prints
    four assorted green prints
    four assorted red/pink/
       purple prints
    one gold/tan print
    one orange print
    one yellow print

Borders:

1¼ yards purple

⅔ yard multi pink/gold

⅔ yard red

⅜ yard light gold

⅜ yard pink

⅜ yard medium gold

⅜ yard multi pink/purple

⅜ yard rust

Also:

½ yard black for binding

4¼ yards backing

74" x 74" batting

Cutting

RADIANT BEAUTY BLOCKS (16)

Use the patterns on pages 46–47, enlarging as indicated. Prepare 8 B and 8 Br paper-piecing patterns. Prepare freezer paper patterns A, Ar, C, Cr, D, Dr, E, and Er.

From the green frog print, cut 8 A and 8 Ar.

From the muted green and the green/brown print, cut sixteen 3¾" x 42" strips total for B and Br.

From the two purples, cut twelve 3" x 42" strips total for B and Br.

From the yellow, cut four 3" x 42" strips total for B and Br.

From two red/pink prints, cut 2 C and 1 Cr. From the other two red/pink prints, cut 1 C and 2 Cr.

From two green prints, cut 2 D and 1 Dr. From the other two green prints, cut 1 D and 2 Dr.

From two red/purple/pink prints, cut 2 E and 1 Er. From the other two red/purple/pink prints, cut 1 E and 2 Er.

From the gold/tan print, cut 2 C and 2 Cr.

From the orange print, cut 2 D and 2 Dr.

From the yellow print, cut 2 E and 2 Er.

Sort the pieces by block, matching the colors.

Radiant Beauty Quilting Design
Enlarge as desired

BORDERS

From each border fabric, cut eight 42"-long strips at the widths listed below. Sew into eight long strips, one per color. Cut into the following border strips:

four 1½" x 75" light gold (A)

four 1½" x 75" pink (B)

four 2½" x 75" multi pink/gold (C)

four 1½" x 75" medium gold (D)

four 2½" x 75" red (E)

four 1½" x 75" multi pink/purple (F)

four 1½" x 75" rust (G)

four 4½" x 75" purple (H)

Assembly

1. Refer to Paper-Piecing an Arc (page 10) and Paper-Piecing Irregular Points (page 42). Make 6 B and 6 Br arcs with purple points and muted green and green/brown backgrounds. Make 2 B and 2 Br arcs with yellow points and green/brown backgrounds. Try to vary the fabric coloration from point to point, as shown in the quilt photograph (page 40).

2. Refer to Joining Curved Sections (page 11). Sew the C, D, and E and the Cr, Dr, and Er pieces together. Use the red/pink, green, and red/purple/pink prints to make four sets of three, or 12 total (six in reverse). Use the gold/tan, orange, and yellow prints to make four total (two in reverse).

3. Sew the A, B, and CDE units together. Make 12 red/green/purple blocks (reverse six) and four yellow/green blocks (reverse two).

4. Lay out the blocks in four rows of four blocks each, placing the arcs and colors as shown in the quilt photograph (page 40) and quilt diagram. Stitch the blocks together in rows. Press. Join the rows. Press.

5. Lay out border strips A through H side by side in order. Stitch A and B together along the long edges. Press toward B. Stitch C to AB. Press toward C. Continue adding the strips in order, pressing after each addition. Make four borders total, each 13½" x 75". Refer to Making Mitered Corners (page 37) to attach and complete the borders.

6. Layer and quilt as desired.

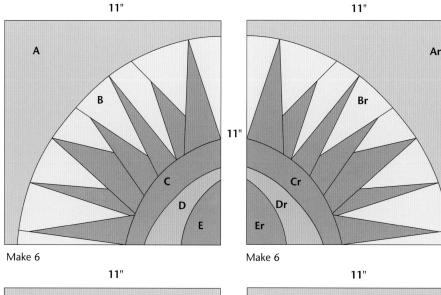

Make 6   Make 6

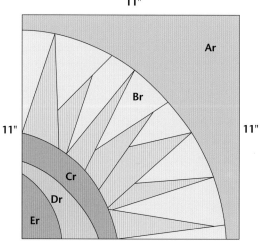

Make 2
Radiant Beauty Blocks

Make 2
Radiant Beauty Reverse Blocks

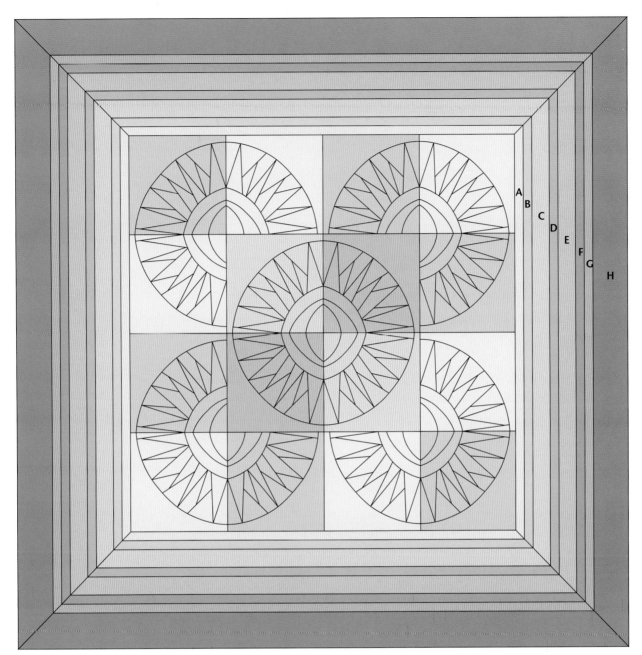

QUILT DIAGRAM

Block Key

▨	Radiant Beauty block
▢	Radiant Beauty reverse block
▨	Radiant Beauty block
▨	Radiant Beauty reverse block

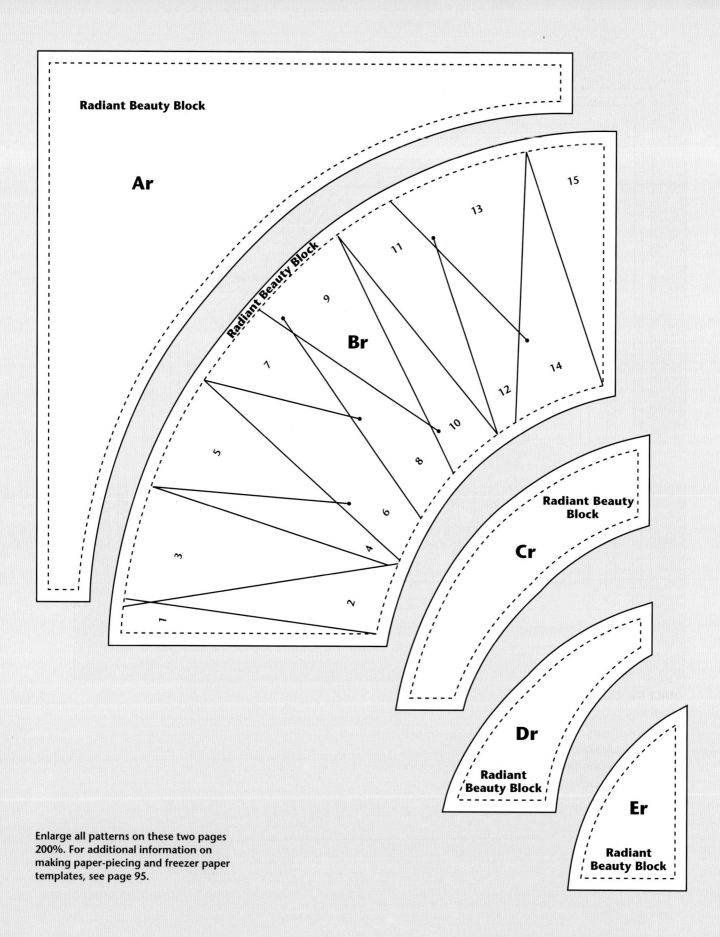

Radiant Beauty Block

Ar

Radiant Beauty Block

Br

7

9

11

13

15

5

8

10

12

14

3

4

6

1

2

Radiant Beauty Block

Cr

Dr

Radiant Beauty Block

Er

Radiant Beauty Block

Enlarge all patterns on these two pages
200%. For additional information on
making paper-piecing and freezer paper
templates, see page 95.

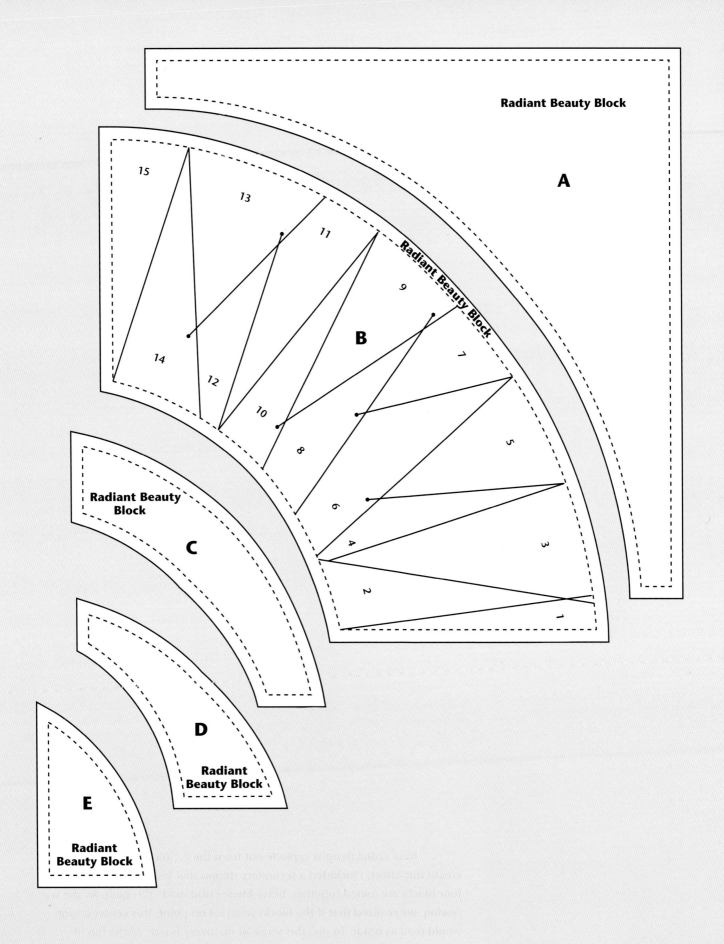

Radiant Beauty Block

A

15
13
11
9
Radiant Beauty Block
14
7
12
B
10
5
8
6
4
3
2
1

Radiant Beauty
Block

C

D

Radiant
Beauty Block

E

Radiant
Beauty Block

Fireworks
in the Garden

hese radial designs explode out from the center, like fireworks. To create this effect, I included a secondary design that becomes visible when four blocks are joined together. Betsy Mennesson made this quilt. As she was sewing, we realized that if the blocks were set on point, this center design would read as a star. To me, this sense of discovery is part of the fun of creating your own blocks. Block size: 12" x 12". Quilt size: 68" x 68".

Fireworks in the Garden
Quilting Design (block center)
Enlarge as desired

Fabric Selection

Betsy agreed to make this quilt even before I chose the fabrics. I got to thinking about the exploding star effect I wanted to create and realized that the palette had to be simple to carry out my idea. When I found a Kaffe Fassett floral that was bright and playful, I knew immediately that Betsy would have fun making the quilt.

The floral print gave me clues for the other fabrics. For the points, I chose a red-orange print that made the reds in the Kaffe Fassett fabric appear even brighter. The background became a soft yellow plaid. Normally, I wouldn't choose a print for the points unless the background was solid, but this combination worked. The yellow set off the points and encircled them, but without sharp or jarring contrast. For the star at the center, I found a red-orange solid and a soft green to surround it.

When Betsy and I got to laying out the blocks, we auditioned lots of fabrics for the setting triangles—greens, oranges, yellows—but none of them worked. The Kaffe Fassett print turned out to be the best solution. With the background extended, the stars seemed to float on the surface. This was another one of those times in quiltmaking when not all the answers are there in the beginning. You have to wait until the quilt talks to you.

Quilting

Betsy took what she has learned from my machine quilting style to produce this beautiful New York Beauty quilt. She developed the garden and fireworks themes already present in the quilt to come up with her own unique quilting patterns. The centers where four blocks meet are quilted with a spiral of circles and leaves. The points are quilted with wavy lines, reminding me of flames. Spiraling circles fill the yellow backgrounds and look equally interesting on the back side of the quilt. To finish off the floral background fabric, Betsy quilted a continuous leaf pattern.

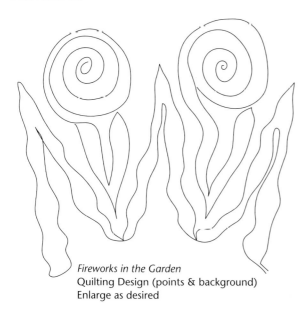

Fireworks in the Garden
Quilting Design (points & background)
Enlarge as desired

Materials

4⅛ yards floral theme print

3¼ yards yellow plaid

2½ yards red-orange print

⅝ yard soft green print

⅜ yard red-orange solid

½ yard for binding

4⅛ yards backing

72" x 72" batting

Cutting

FIREWORKS BLOCKS (24)

Use the patterns on page 52, enlarging as indicated. Prepare 24 B and 24 C paper-piecing patterns. Prepare freezer paper pattern A.

From the floral theme print, cut 24 A.

From the yellow plaid, cut thirty-two 3½" x 42" strips for B.

From the red-orange print, cut thirty-four 2½" x 42" strips for B.

From the red-orange solid, cut three 3" x 42" strips for C.

From the soft green, cut five 3½" x 42" strips for C.

SETTING TRIANGLES

From the floral theme print, cut one 18¼" x 42" strip. Cut into two 18¼" squares. Cut diagonally in both directions for eight setting triangles. Cut one 17⅞" x 42" strip. Cut into two 17⅞" squares. Cut diagonally in half for four corner setting triangles.

Assembly

1. Refer to Paper-Piecing an Arc (page 10) and Paper-Piecing Irregular Points (page 42). Make 24 B arcs with red-orange print points and yellow plaid backgrounds. Make 24 C arcs with red-orange in the middle and green at the sides.

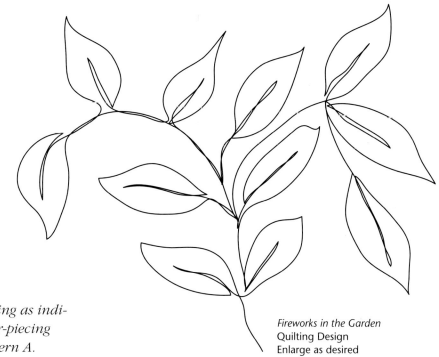

Fireworks in the Garden
Quilting Design
Enlarge as desired

2. Refer to Joining Curved Sections (page 11). Join A, B, and C to make 24 blocks.

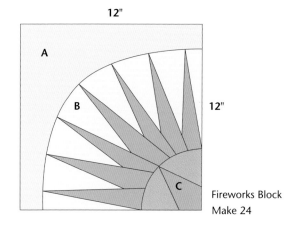

Fireworks Block
Make 24

3. Lay out the blocks on point as shown in the quilt photograph (page 48) and quilt diagram. Add the setting triangles. Stitch the blocks and setting triangles together in diagonal rows. Press. Join the rows. Press. Add the corner triangles last. Press.

4. Layer and quilt as desired.

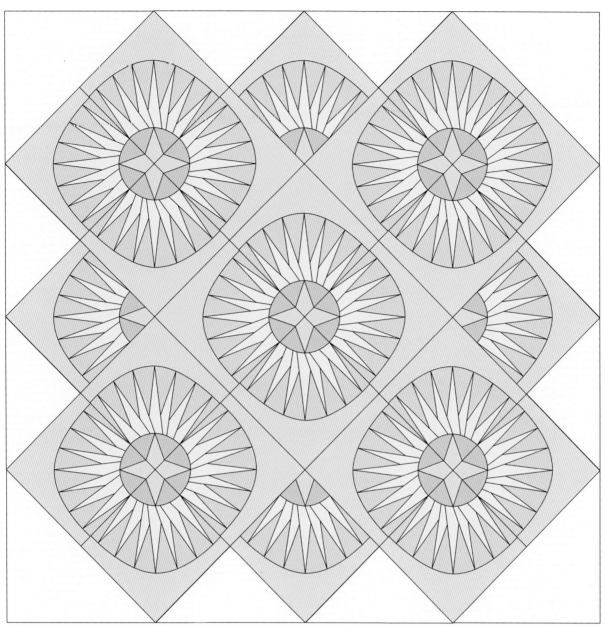

QUILT DIAGRAM

Right: Even dried plants can offer
design ideas and color palettes

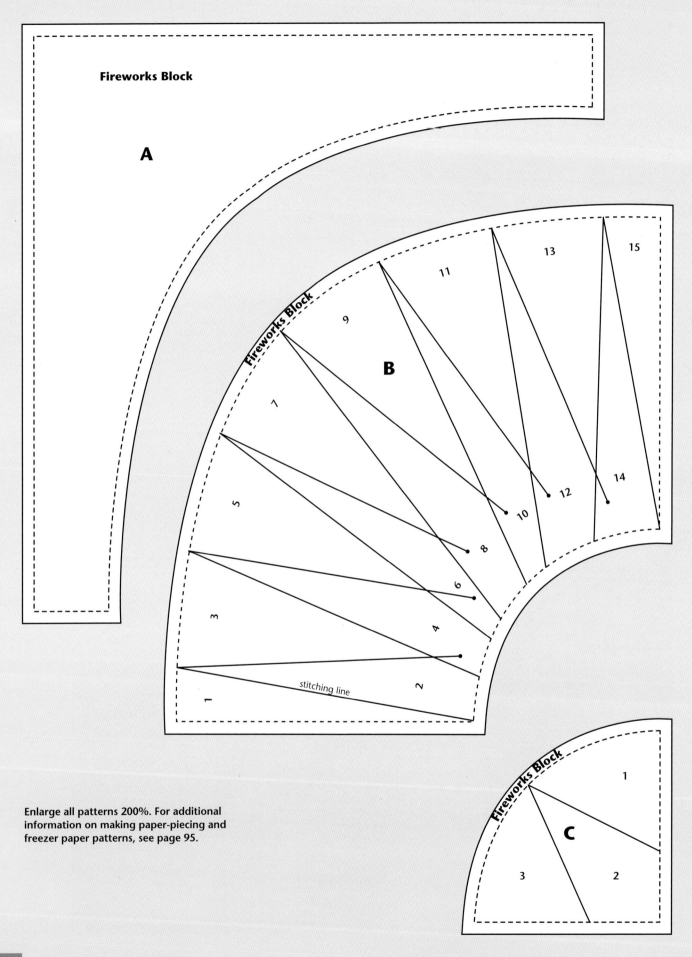

Fireworks Block

A

Fireworks Block

B

9

11

13

15

7

5

3

12

10

8

6

4

14

stitching line

2

1

Enlarge all patterns 200%. For additional information on making paper-piecing and freezer paper patterns, see page 95.

Fireworks Block

C

1

3

2

Aria

ectangular New York Beauty blocks make *Aria* unique. Assembled from just four blocks, this small quilt would make a special baby gift. The blocks are made in mirror image pairs so that the irregular arc patterns match up at the seams. The inner hub of each arc features several curved sections. When each section is pieced from a different fabric, the patterns and colors play off one another and rev up the palette. Check out the Quilting section on page 54 for tips on big-stitch folk art hand quilting. Block size: 12½" x 15½". Quilt size: 38" x 44".

Fabric Selection

My new collection of batiks had just arrived at the store, and I needed a quilt design to showcase the fabric. *Aria* was drafted specifically for this purpose. While working on the quilt, I realized it would look great in other fabric styles too.

The four blocks are arranged so that the arcs form an oval. To make the palette come together, I grouped the fabrics by color. I chose yellow for the center but debated between yellow and pink for the points. Yellow was the more obvious choice, but it seemed too predictable. The pink was bright and threw off the same sort of glow as the yellow, so I figured, why not?

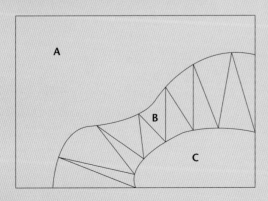

There are a lot of possibilities for color in this quilt. The curved arcs at the center lend themselves to prints and connect with one another, creating multicolor rings. The border colors are also closely related. Deep purple and yellow inner borders give way to a wider multicolor outer border, adding to the continuity of the quilt. I like the way touches of yellow in the outer border fabric bounce the eye back to the yellow at the center of the quilt.

Quilting

This quilt seemed to say, "Please don't machine-quilt me." Perhaps it was because I had recently seen larger-stitch hand quilting on some folk art quilts and found it very attractive. I decided to give it a try.

It can be tough to hand-quilt batiks because of the dense weave. A larger stitch and needle helped overcome this obstacle. I used YLI Jeans Stitch thread, which is thicker than normal hand quilting or machine quilting thread, and a Clover Sashico needle. I quilted around the points, did small swirls in the background, followed the curves at the center of the quilt, and worked straight lines in the borders. Next time around, I'm going to trim away the excess fabric from the back of the block before I layer and baste the quilt. Even with my big-stitch method, those multiple fabric layers were difficult to stitch through.

Big-stitch quilting gives the quilt a gentle drape and soft handmade feel. I really like the tactile quality this type of hand stitching brings to the quilt.

MINI LESSON *Drafting a Freestyle Block*

No compass needed here! Freestyle New York Beauty blocks have gentle curves that seem to flow through the block. The block can be square or rectangular. To draft your own version, you'll need a ruler, a pencil, graph paper, and a flexible curve ruler.

1. Draft a square or rectangle the size of the finished block on the graph paper.

2. Decide on the general size of the outermost arc. It can cover a larger or smaller area of the block, as you choose. Measure from two opposite corners down to where you want the arc to begin. Mark a point at each spot. Don't worry about symmetry or connecting the arcs at this point.

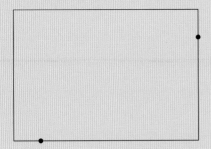

3. Place the flexible curve ruler on the drawing. This plastic bendable ruler is ¼" wide and 18" long. Align the edge of the ruler on each point and shape the section of the ruler in between any way you like. The curve can be smooth or wavy. When you've got it where you want it, trace along the edge of the ruler with a pencil.

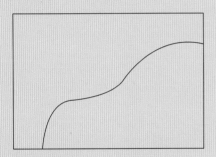

4. Repeat steps 2 and 3 to mark additional curved arcs as desired. As you can see from the quilts in this book, there are many possibilities.

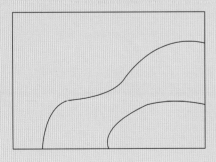

5. Use a pencil and a straight-edged ruler to draw points for paper piecing inside one or more of the arcs. Making the points different widths and heights will accentuate the irregularity of the arcs. You can also make points overlap one another at the base. Think outside the box!

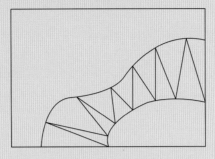

6. When you're satisfied with your block pattern, label each section A, B, C, etc. Think through the paper-piecing sequence, and number the points and background points.

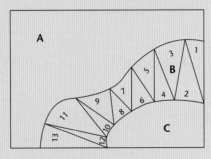

7. Lay a sheet of tracing paper on top of the block pattern. Use your rulers and a pencil to trace the entire block design. Turn the tracing over and go over the traced lines from the wrong side. Add the labels Ar, Br, Cr, etc., and number the points. You now have a mirror image copy of the block pattern. Both versions, used together, will allow your irregular arc designs to connect at the seams when two or more blocks are joined together.

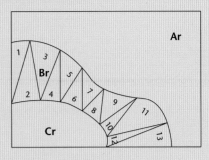

8. Trace sections A, B, C, etc., of each block individually. Use the ¼"-wide flexible curve ruler to add a ¼" seam allowance all around. Label each pattern. Use the patterns to make paper-piecing patterns and freezer paper patterns as appropriate.

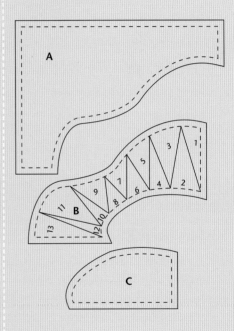

Materials

Use batik fabrics.

Blocks:

1 yard pink

½ yard blue

½ yard green

½ yard tan/purple/blue

½ yard purple

Scraps (12" x 12"):
   blue-green
   olive green
   yellow/purple
   gray/purple
   tan

Borders:

⅜ yard dark purple/burgundy

⅜ yard orange/purple/burgundy

¼ yard yellow

Also:

¼ yard for binding

1½ yards backing

42" x 48" batting

Cutting

ARIA BLOCKS (4)

Use the patterns on pages 58–59, enlarging as indicated. Prepare 4 B and 4 Br paper-piecing patterns. Prepare freezer paper patterns A, Ar, C, Cr, D, Dr, E, Er, F, and Fr.

From the blue and the green batiks, cut 1 A and 1 C each. Cut the remainder into 4"-wide strips for B.

From the tan/purple/blue and the purple batiks, cut 1 Ar and 1 Cr each. Cut the remainder into 4"-wide strips for Br.

From the pink batik, cut seven 3½" x 42" strips for B and Br.

From the blue-green and the olive green batiks, cut 1 D each.

From the yellow/purple and gray/purple batiks, cut 1 Dr each.

From the tan batik, cut 2 E and 2 Er.

From the yellow batik, cut 2 F and 2 Fr.

Sort the pieces by block, referring to the quilt photograph (page 53).

BORDERS

From the dark purple/burgundy batik, cut three 2½" x 42" strips. Sew into one long strip. Cut into two 2½" x 31½" strips for the side inner borders and two 2½" x 29½" strips for the top and bottom inner borders.

From the yellow batik, cut four 1" x 42" strips. Sew into one long strip. Cut into two 1" x 35½" strips for the side middle borders and two 1" x 30½" strips for the top and bottom middle borders.

From the orange/purple/burgundy batik, cut three 4½" x 42" strips. Sew into one long strip. Cut into two 4½" x 36½" strips for the side outer borders and two 4½" x 38½" strips for the top and bottom outer borders.

Assembly

1. Refer to Paper-Piecing an Arc (page 10) and Paper-Piecing Irregular Points (page 42). Make 2 B and 2 Br arcs with pink batik points. Give each arc a different background: blue, green, tan/purple/blue, or purple.

2. Refer to Joining Curved Sections (page 11). Join A to B and Ar to Br, matching the background colors. Join C, D, E, and F and Cr, Dr, Er, and Fr. Join the units together so that the background colors match and the pink points appear to float. Make four blocks total (two in reverse).

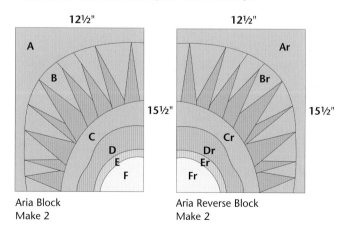

Aria Block
Make 2

Aria Reverse Block
Make 2

3. Lay out the blocks in two rows of two to form a starburst, as shown in the quilt photograph (page 53) and quilt diagram. Stitch the blocks together in rows. Press. Join the rows. Press.

4. Sew the side inner borders to the quilt top. Press toward the borders. Add the top and bottom inner borders. Press. Add the middle and outer borders in the same sequence, pressing after each addition.

5. Layer and quilt as desired.

Above: This is a twig tree that I stood over and got in close to photograph. There are so many ways to look at objects—under, over, sideways. Sometimes it's just a matter of taking the time to see.

QUILT DIAGRAM

Block Key

▭ Aria block
▥ Aria reverse block

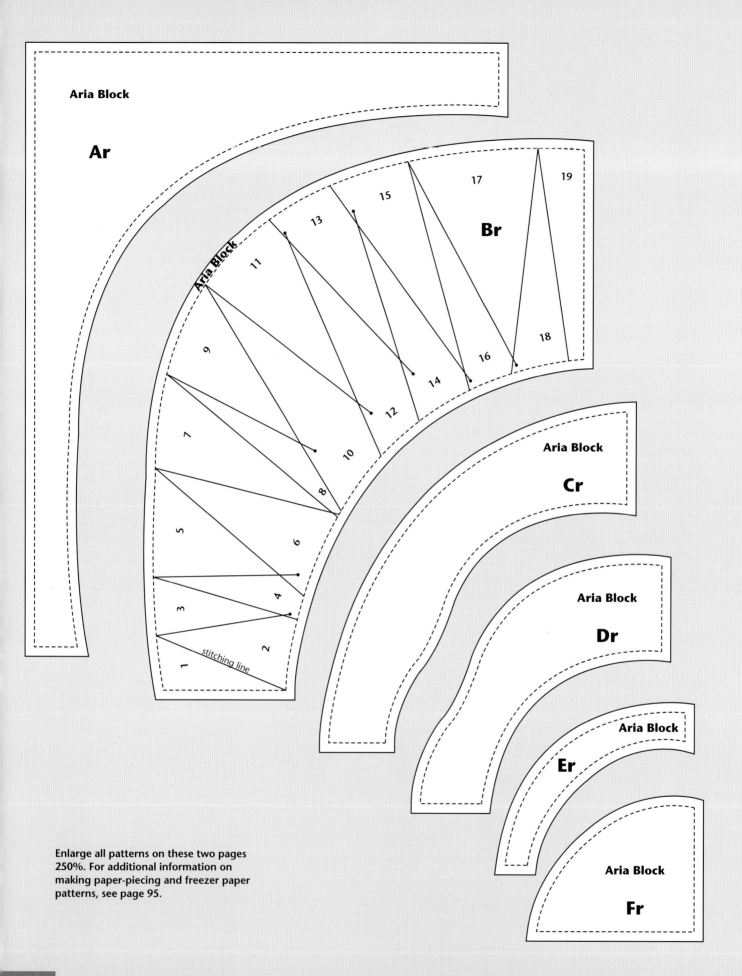

Aria Block

Ar

Aria Block

Br

11 13 15 17 19

9 12 14 16 18

7 10

8

5 6

3 4

1 2

stitching line

Aria Block

Cr

Aria Block

Dr

Aria Block

Er

Aria Block

Fr

Enlarge all patterns on these two pages 250%. For additional information on making paper-piecing and freezer paper patterns, see page 95.

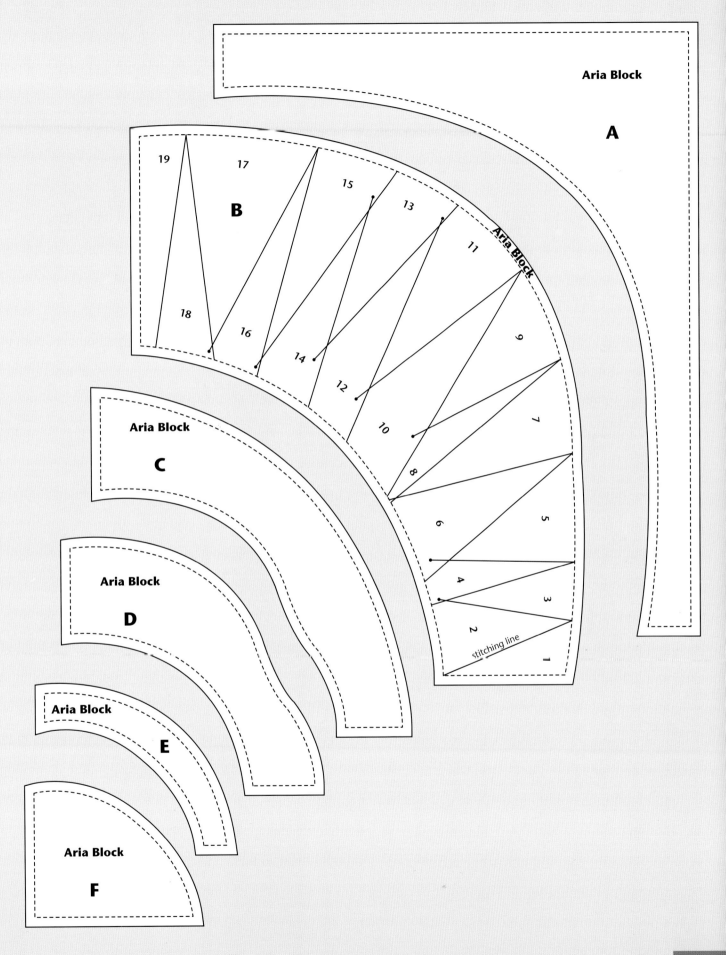

Aria Block

A

Aria Block

B

19
17
15
13
11
18
16
14
12
10
9
8
7
6
5
4
3
2
1

stitching line

Aria Block

C

Aria Block

D

Aria Block

E

Aria Block

F

Sunday Morning

Sunday Morning is a large bed-size version of *Aria* made by Barbara Ferguson. It contains sixteen Aria blocks. To make the block larger without changing the arc size, we simply extended pattern piece A to the required dimensions. One reason for the increased size was to accommodate the large floral print chosen for the background. Colors for the companion fabrics were pulled from this old-fashioned print. This quilt shows how interpreting a block with a different combination of fabrics can change the look entirely. Block size: 13½" x 16½". Quilt size: 80" x 92".

Fabric Selection

Quiltmaker Barbara Ferguson and I decided to make a large vintage floral our guide for this quilt. We liked the green, red, and yellow hues in the print and looked for companion fabrics in the same colors. We also wanted the companion fabrics to keep the same vintage feel.

We ended up with an assortment of different reds, greens, and creams, which we used to create the arc points and backgrounds as well as the plain arcs and center pieces. The reds range in scale and style of print. Some are compact, others are open. We included plaids, medium-size florals, and even a solid. If you don't have scraps to pick through, fat quarters are a good way to assemble such a wide-ranging palette.

It's important to push the color in several directions. Our creams, for instance, include cool beige, warm soft yellow, and even an open floral print with the same red as the point fabrics. We chose a more intense green floral with similar reds for the center of the blocks.

Laying out the fabrics was a real eye-opener. Reds that were more intense than the floral theme print actually made the print more vibrant and made the points pop out. A couple of fabrics seemed to stand out too much, but they were needed. Barbara made the statement that you always need a little "pucker" to make the quilt work.

Working from a single theme fabric means finding all of the other fabric clues within it. It can be a challenge to find the pucker fabric—the one that doesn't seem right but that in small quantities will make the quilt sing. Yellow is the pucker fabric in *Sunday Morning*. You have to look hard to find the yellow in the theme print, but the narrow yellow arcs bring the blocks to life. It is important to listen to the fabric when making a quilt with a theme print.

Quilting

Sunday Morning was quilted from the back, using the backing fabric—the same floral print that appears on the quilt top—as a guide. This is a great way to get comfortable with free-motion quilting since you have a design to follow.

Barbara prepared the backing by cutting three panels of the print and sewing them together. Then she layered the quilt upside down, with the quilt top on the bottom and the backing on top. The pin-basting was done from the backing side too. Barbara followed the design within the floral fabric, adding a few leaves of her own. One of the beautiful things that happens when you quilt from the back is that the stitching design that appears on the front has a random relationship to the pieced top.

Materials

Blocks:

3 yards red/white floral theme print

Fat quarters (18" x 22"):
 10 assorted red plaids and prints
 10 assorted cream plaids and prints
 1 brown/red/green floral print

⅛ yard each nine assorted green prints, plaids, and textured solids

Scraps (12" x 12") of six assorted gold prints, plaids, and textured solids

Borders:

2⅞ yards red/white floral theme print

¾ yard green textured solid

1 yard red print

Also:

⅔ yard for binding

7⅛ yards backing

84" x 96" batting

Cutting

LARGE ARIA BLOCKS (16)

Use the patterns on pages 58–59 and 64–65, enlarging as indicated. Prepare 8 B and 8 Br paper-piecing patterns. Prepare freezer paper patterns AA, AAr, C, Cr, D, Dr, E, Er, F, and Fr.

From the red/white floral theme print, cut 8 AA and 8 AAr.

From the assorted reds, cut a total of forty-eight 3½" x 18" strips for B and Br.

From the assorted creams, cut a total of fifty-four 4" x 18" strips for B and Br.

From the assorted greens, cut 8 C, 8 Cr, 8 D, and 8 Dr.

From the assorted golds, cut 8 E and 8 Er.

From the brown/red/green floral print, cut 8 F and 8 Fr. The pieces in *Sunday Morning* were fussy-cut so that the green falls along the curved edge.

BORDERS

From the green textured solid, cut nine 2½" x 42" strips. Sew into one long strip. Cut into two 2½" x 96" strips for the side inner borders and two 2½" x 84" strips for the top and bottom inner borders.

From the red print, cut nine 3½" x 42" strips. Sew into one long strip. Cut into two 3½" x 96" strips for the side middle borders and two 3½" x 84" strips for the top and bottom middle borders.

From the red/white floral print, cut on the lengthwise grain two 8½" x 96" strips for the side outer borders and two 8½" x 84" strips for the top and bottom outer borders.

Assembly

1. Refer to Paper-Piecing an Arc (page 10) and Paper-Piecing Irregular Points (page 42). Make 8 B and 8 Br arcs with assorted red points and assorted cream backgrounds.

2. Refer to Joining Curved Sections (page 11). Join AA to B and AAr to Br, matching the background colors. Join C, D, E, and F and Cr, Dr, Er, and Fr, referring to the quilt photograph (page 60) for color placement ideas. Join the units together to make 16 blocks total (eight in reverse).

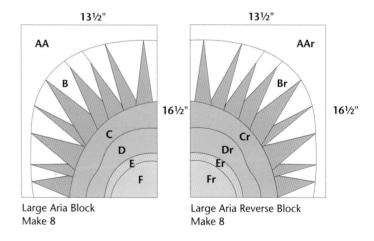

Large Aria Block
Make 8

Large Aria Reverse Block
Make 8

3. Lay out the blocks in four rows of four blocks each, as shown in the quilt photograph (page 60) and quilt diagram. Stitch the blocks together in rows. Press. Join the rows. Press.

4. Sew the inner, middle, and outer side border strips together along the long edges. Press toward the outer border. Repeat to make two side and two top and bottom borders, each 13½" wide. Refer to Making Mitered Corners (page 37) to attach and complete the borders.

5. Layer and quilt as desired.

Above: I love this vase and the way the crackle of the glaze moves within the vertical curves.

QUILT DIAGRAM

Block Key

Large Aria block

Large Aria reverse block

Large Aria Block

AAr

Enlarge patterns AA and AAr 200%. For the remaining block patterns, see pages 58–59. For additional information on making paper-piecing and freezer paper patterns, see page 95.

Above and right: Old Victorian houses offer lots of radiating designs for the discerning viewer.

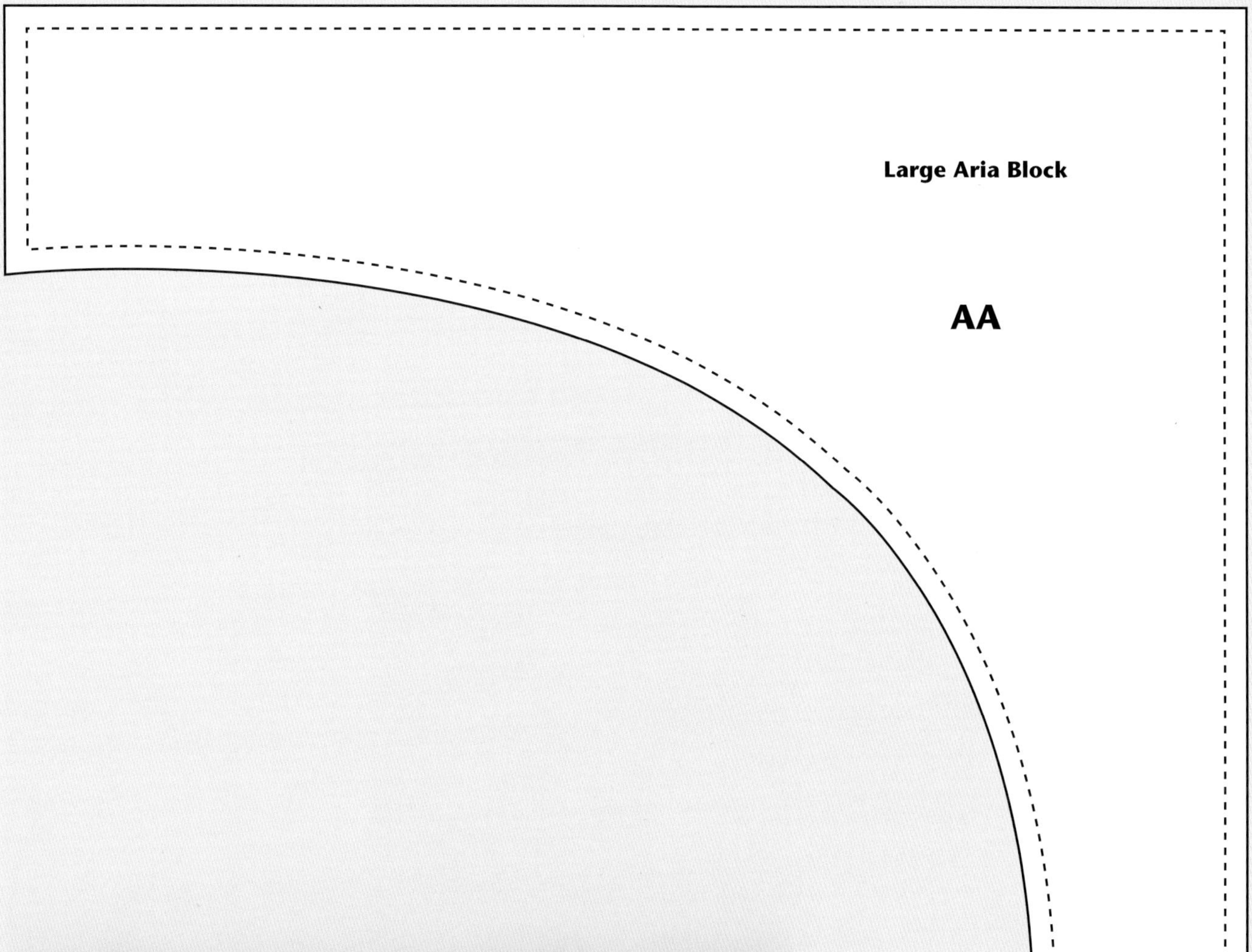

Large Aria Block

AA

Pacific Rim

acific Rim is a contemporary quilt with Asian flare. The fabric colors and prints carry out the Asian theme, as do the open circles in the design. The circles are created by omitting the paper-pieced points and cutting the arcs from a single fabric instead. Around the time I was developing this idea, I saw a guild exhibit based on circle designs. There were numerous quilts with an Asian feel that fell into what I was striving to create here. Since the paper-pieced block sections were busy to look at and labor-intensive to make, I limited their number. A black border contains the blocks and adds a note of serenity. Block size: 12" x 12". Quilt size: 64" x 64".

Fabric Selection

This quilt started with a red fabric that mixed large Asian figures with graphic designs. I had the fabric for almost a year before I designed the block and found a way to handle this larger motif. As I collected more motif fabrics in reds and blacks, my palette began to emerge. Blue accents appeared in some of the prints, so I started collecting blue-and-white prints, also with an Asian flare, for the points.

My original plan was to paper-piece both the A section and the B arc with long narrow points. But when I put these two pieced sections together, the block became far too busy. The pieces competed with one another, and their unique quality disappeared. To remedy the situation, I separated the pieced sections and paired each one with a compatible print instead. Fussy-cutting ensured that all the print motifs faced the same way once the quilt was assembled.

The blue used in the points appears in other areas too, gently pulling the eye across the surface of the quilt. I used small amounts of gold to accent the blue points. For a true sparkle effect, it's important to keep the dosage low.

This block design and layout could easily be translated into florals, for a garden-style quilt, or plaids and stripes, for a geometric interpretation.

Quilting

As I pieced the blocks together, I contemplated how I was going to quilt them. With such a variety of motif prints playing off one another, I needed to find a common denominator that would represent the quilt as a whole. I decided on bamboo, bamboo leaves, and circles. The circles would echo the circles that were created within the quilt blocks during the piecing.

The bamboo stalks start at the bottom of the quilt and go completely off the top, adding subtle linear dimension. Leaves grow off the bamboo at random. The spaces that are left are filled in with circles. I chose a thread color that would show up in some spots and blend in with the quilt in others. By taking clues from the individual fabrics as well as the overall mood of the quilt, I found my quilting designs.

Pacific Rim Quilting Design
Enlarge as desired

Materials

Use Asian-themed fabrics.

3⅜ yards total assorted blue prints

2⅜ yards total assorted red prints

⅞ yard red geometric print

⅞ yard black landscape print

⅝ yard red/black motif print

⅜ yard red calligraphy print

⅜ yard black mountains print

⅜ yard red crane print

⅜ yard black/red dragon print

¼ yard blue/black print

¼ yard black/red calligraphy print

¼ yard black/red/blue print

¼ yard gold print

⅛ yard light red print

⅞ yard black (includes ⅜ yard for binding)

3¾ yards backing

68" x 68" batting

Cutting

PACIFIC RIM BLOCKS (25)

Use the patterns on page 70, enlarging as indicated. Prepare 6 A and 10 B paper-piecing patterns. Prepare freezer paper patterns A, B, and C. Refer to the block orientation in the quilt diagram to fussy-cut the A's and B's.

From the red geometric print, cut 4 A.

From the black landscape print, cut 4 A.

From the red calligraphy print, cut 3 A.

From the red/black motif print, cut 2 A and 4 B.

From the black mountains print, cut 2 A and 2 B.

From the red crane print, cut 2 A.

From the black/red dragon print, cut 2 A.

From the blue/black print, cut 4 B.

From the black/red calligraphy print, cut 3 B.

From the black/red/blue print, cut 2 B.

From the assorted blue prints, cut 14 C.

From a light red print, cut 11 C.

Cut the gold and the remaining blue prints into 2½"-wide strips for A and B.

Cut the remaining red prints into 2"-wide strips for A and B.

BORDER

From the black solid, cut six 2½" x 42" strips. Sew into one long strip. Cut into two 2½" x 60½" strips for the top and bottom borders and two 2½" x 64½" strips for the side borders. Set aside the remaining black for the binding.

Assembly

1. Refer to Paper-Piecing an Arc (page 10) and Paper-Piecing Irregular Points (page 42). Make 6 A arcs and 6 B arcs with blue points and red backgrounds. Include two or three gold points among the blues in each piece. Make 4 B arcs with red points and blue backgrounds.

2. Refer to Joining Curved Sections (page 11). Join the pieced arcs and solid pieces A, B, and C, referring to the quilt diagram for the fabric and color combinations. Make 25 blocks total.

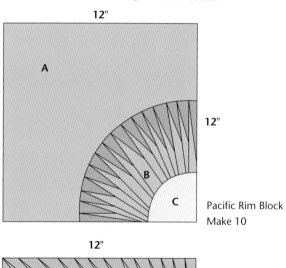

Pacific Rim Block
Make 10

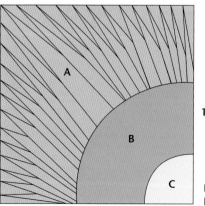

Pacific Rim Block
Make 6

12"

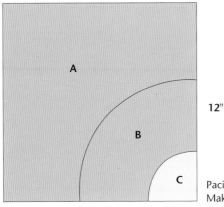

12"

Pacific Rim Block
Make 9

3. Lay out the blocks in five rows of five blocks each, as shown in the quilt photograph (page 66) and quilt diagram. Stitch the blocks together in rows. Press. Join the rows. Press.

4. Sew the top and bottom borders to the quilt top. Press. Add the side borders. Press.

5. Layer and quilt as desired.

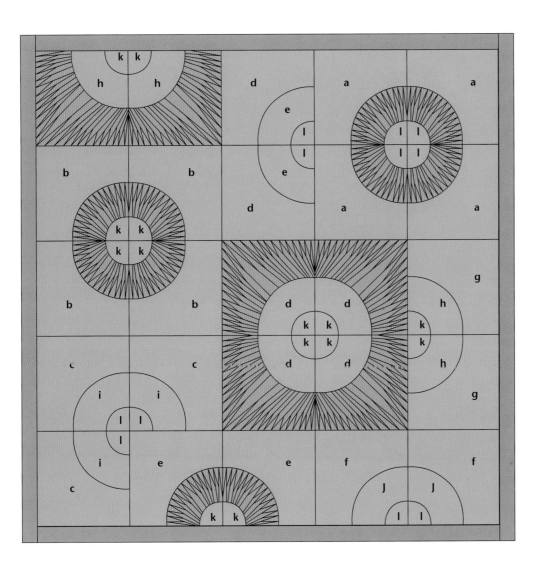

QUILT DIAGRAM

Fabric Key

	pieced arc
a	red geometric print
b	black landscape print
c	red calligraphy print
d	red/black motif print
e	black mountains print
f	red crane print
g	black/red dragon print
h	blue/black print
i	black/red calligraphy print
j	black/red/blue print
k	assorted blue prints
l	light red print

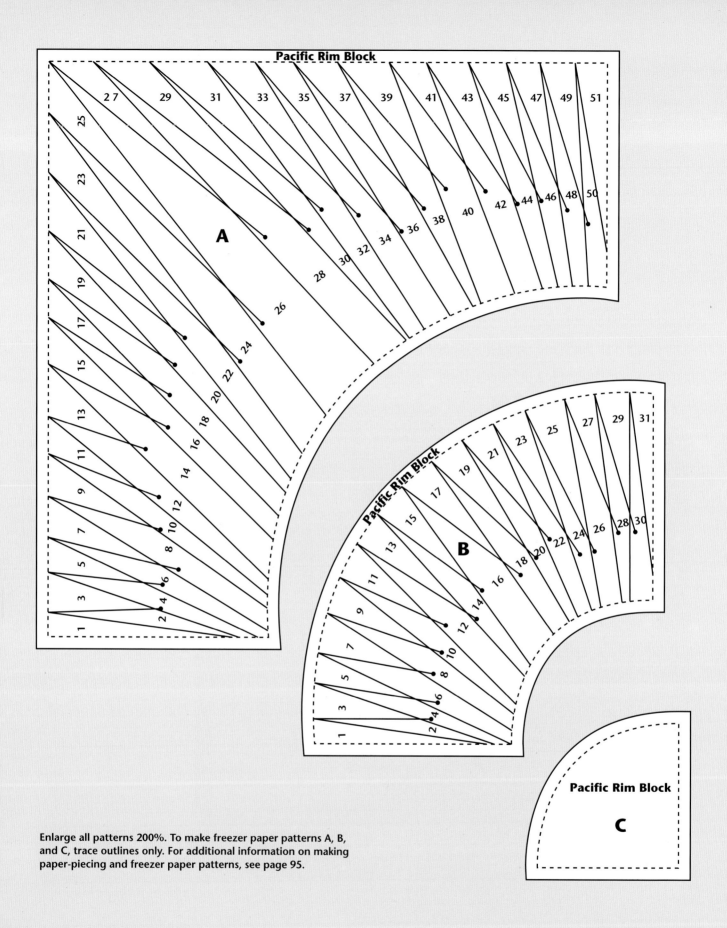

Enlarge all patterns 200%. To make freezer paper patterns A, B, and C, trace outlines only. For additional information on making paper-piecing and freezer paper patterns, see page 95.

Lazy Daisy

This quilt design features a block that I had originally drafted for *Sorbet Sunrise*. I had a new collection of fabric on the market that I couldn't wait to try out. The fabric design is based on Gerber daisies, dahlias, and other garden plants and objects. I love the Gerber daisy with its abundant overlapping petals. This block seemed to be the perfect design to mimic the flower and the fabric motifs and bring everything full circle. I believe that quiltmakers should use their creative license to push the design envelope and come up with unique interpretations. To someone else, these blocks may not look like daisies, but that doesn't bother me. My goal was to combine fabric and quilting into an artistic representation. That is part of the beauty of quilting to me. Block sizes: 5" x 8" and 5" x 4". Quilt size: 52" x 52".

gained a delicate but decisive frame. Keep this option in mind for the next time you feel stumped by a binding. All aspects of the quilt, including the binding, affect how the quilt appears visually.

Quilting

To follow through on the daisy theme, I quilted petal shapes within the blocks, filling as much of the rectangle as possible. I used variegated thread that weaved in and out among the multiple colors radiating from the center of each flower.

Once I had all of the flowers done, I took a look at the sashing. I wanted something understated and subtle. I found a great soft variegated thread that contained all the colors in the print. I decided on a swirls. The easygoing continuous design was simple to quilt. It didn't detract from the flowers in the print, but it also fit into the stylized mood set by the daisies.

Fabric Selection

Most of the fabrics in this quilt are from a collection of my own designs. They include florals and monochromatic geometrics in a variety of hues, including grassy green, olive, purple, violet, pink, peach, and bright orange. I added a few hand-dyed fabrics to settle down the livelier prints. I found that when I included a more subtle print or solid in these pieced blocks, the prints became more interesting.

Four different blocks are used in *Lazy Daisy*, although they appear like much more. By combining them in different ways, I was able to come up with different sizes and shapes for the flower units. As a general rule, I tried to put brighter or lighter colors toward the top of each flower and darker fabrics toward the base. Both values fill in the middle, and there are plenty of exceptions to keep things lively. Keeping the palette rich with color fulfilled the idea in my mind of a garden bursting with lazy daisy blooms. The irregular layout of the units also mimics a casual, lushly growing garden. I chose a single theme print for the irregular sashing to tie all the units together.

One of my more important fabric choices in this quilt was the binding color. The quilt didn't need a border since the sashing went all around, but it still needed to be contained. By repeating one of the darkest quilt colors in the binding, the entire piece

Lazy Daisy Quilting Designs
Enlarge as desired

Sashing can rescue New York Beauty blocks from boredom or liven up a plain setting. Here are some tips and observations to keep in mind as you think through your own sashing design options.

- Use sashing to liven up the setting. The blocks made for *Yee-hah!* (page 34) used a terrific cowgirl theme print, but the print lost impact when all the blocks were laid out side by side. Sashing provided a way to break out the blocks into sections to make the full-, half-, and quarter-circle designs more prominent.

- Pay attention to color. Look for sashing colors that relate to the other fabrics in the quilt or to the overall theme of the quilt. In *Yee-hah!*, red and blue plaid sashing picked up on the cowgirl theme print and on the bandana prints used in the arcs and block centers. In *Lazy Daisy*

(page 71), a theme print was used exclusively for the sashing. In this quilt, the sashing fabric inspired the other fabric choices.

- Audition different strip widths to find the appropriate size for your quilt. The color may be right, but if the strip is too narrow or too wide, you may achieve too little accent or too much. The sashing width should complement and draw attention to the blocks, not become a distraction.

- Be unconventional. The sashing strips in a quilt don't all have to be the same width or length or follow a precise grid layout. The different sizes and shapes of blocks made for *Lazy Daisy* required a special setting to tie them all together. The sashing

became one more piece of the puzzle. It also acted as a border around the edges.

- Play around with sashing ideas. If you like the blocks in a plain setting, audition a few sashing colors anyway. You may find that sashing makes the quilt blocks even more interesting and ties them together in a way you hadn't visualized before. Sashing is an easy addition to make. Take time to think about your sashing options when you are planning a quilt.

Materials

2½ yards total assorted greens

1⅛ yards floral theme print (for sashing)

1 yard total assorted oranges, including peach and bright orange

¾ yard total assorted rusts

¾ yard total assorted purples and violets

⅝ yard total assorted lavenders

⅝ yard total assorted yellows

½ yard total assorted burgundies

⅛ yard pink

¼ yard for binding

3¼ yards backing

56" x 56" batting

Cutting

BLOCKS (60)

Use the patterns on page 76, enlarging as indicated. Prepare 16 A, 16 Ar, 14 B, and 14 Br paper-piecing patterns. Prepare 19 freezer paper templates C for needleturn appliqué (see page 20).

From the assorted fabrics, cut 19 C for the flower center appliqués: 4 purple, 5 burgundy, 1 rust, 1 orange, 6 green, and 2 yellow.

Cut the remaining assorted fabrics plus the pink into 1⅝"-wide strips.

SASHING

From the floral theme print, cut one 3½" x 42" strip, seven 2½" x 42" strips, and eight 1½" x 42" strips. Cut into 51 sashing strips:

three 3½" x 13½" (A)
one 2½" x 23½" (B)
one 2½" x 16½" (C)
six 2½" x 13½" (D)
two 2½" x 12½" (E)
one 2½" x 11½" (F)
four 2½" x 10½" (G)
one 2½" x 8½" (H)
three 2½" x 4½" (I)
two 1½" x 17½" (J)
two 1½" x 16½" (K)
three 1½" x 13½" (L)
five 1½" x 12½" (M)
two 1½" x 11½" (N)
eight 1½" x 10½" (O)
one 1½" x 8½" (P)
six 1½" x 4½" (Q)

Also cut one 4½" x 6½" rectangle (R).

Assembly

1. Refer to Paper-Piecing an Arc (page 10). In this quilt, the paper-pieced blocks are joined together in groups of two or four to make the Lazy Daisy units. Piece the blocks and complete one unit at a time, referring to the quilt photograph (page 71) for color ideas. Various color combinations are used: yellow/peach/orange, green/yellow/olive, violet/peach/purple, green/violet/peach, burgundy/purple/green, and so forth. Make 16 A, 16 Ar, 14 B, and 14 Br blocks. Do not remove the paper patterns.

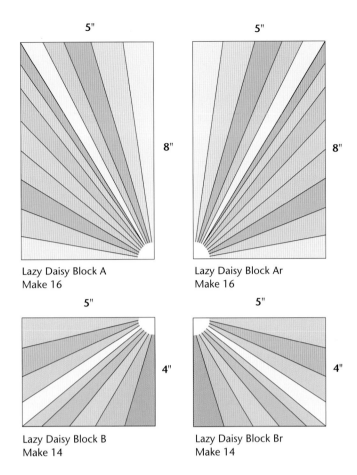

Lazy Daisy Block A
Make 16

Lazy Daisy Block Ar
Make 16

Lazy Daisy Block B
Make 14

Lazy Daisy Block Br
Make 14

2. Trim the corner of each block ¼" beyond the curved dotted line to reduce bulk. Remove the paper patterns.

3. Lay out the blocks in groups of four and two to form 11 radiating daisies and 8 half-daisies, as shown in the quilt photograph (page 71) and quilt diagram. Stitch the blocks together in pairs. Press. Join the pairs indicated to make the full daisy units. Press.

4. Refer to Needleturn Appliqué (page 20). Appliqué piece C in a coordinating color to the center of each daisy. On the half-daisy units, trim off the excess C even with the edge of the blocks.

5. Lay out the daisy units, sashing strips A thru Q, and rectangle R. Stitch the sashing strips and daisy units together, pressing after each addition, to make five sections total. Note that piece B is left unstitched for the last few inches. Sew the sections together in the order shown.

6. Layer and quilt as desired.

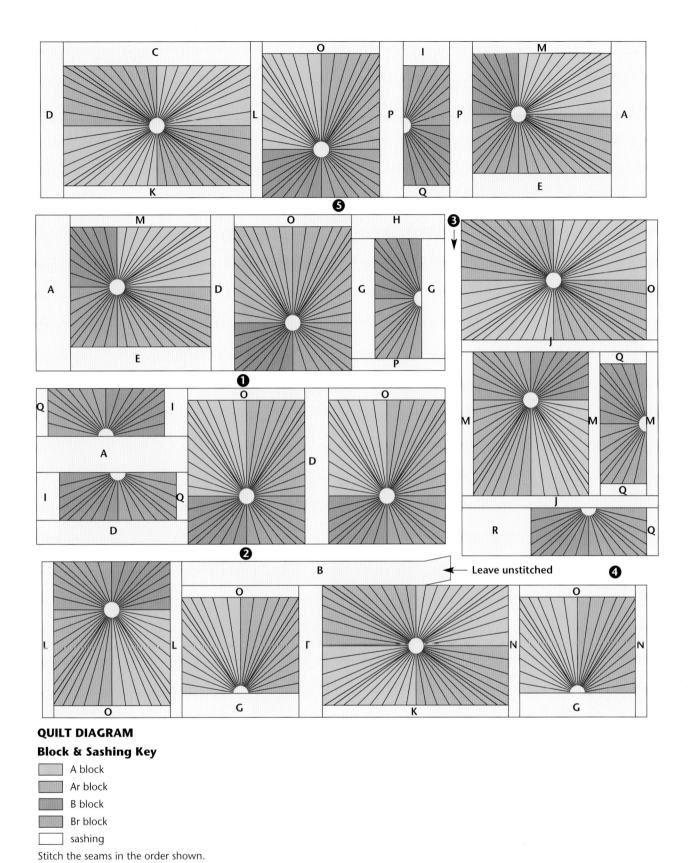

QUILT DIAGRAM

Block & Sashing Key

- A block
- Ar block
- B block
- Br block
- sashing

Stitch the seams in the order shown.

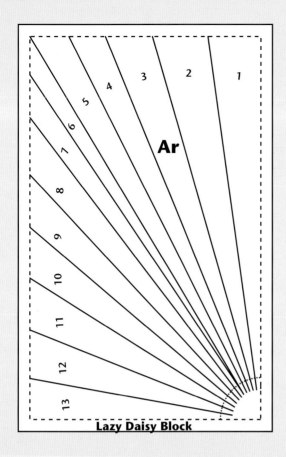

Ar

1 2 3 4 5 6 7 8 9 10 11 12 13

Lazy Daisy Block

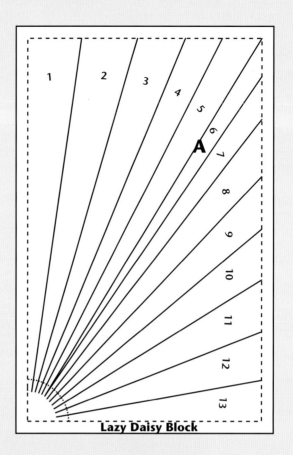

A

1 2 3 4 5 6 7 8 9 10 11 12 13

Lazy Daisy Block

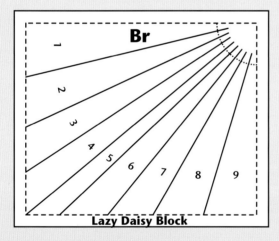

Br

1 2 3 4 5 6 7 8 9

Lazy Daisy Block

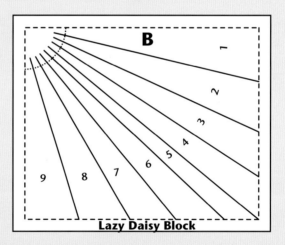

B

1 2 3 4 5 6 7 8 9

Lazy Daisy Block

Enlarge all patterns 200%. For additional
information on making paper-piecing
and freezer paper patterns, see page 95.
For information on freezer paper
appliqué templates, see page 20.

**Lazy Daisy
Block**

C

Cushion
Flowers

ach of the five cushion flowers in this piece designed by my mother, Jean Wells, uses a slightly different palette. The variations are subtle and sophisticated, inviting closer inspection of the batik fabrics. The tall stems and broad leaves are pure fancy, the product of a fertile imagination rather than botanical accuracy. When you are making a quilt, you can design the pieces any way you like. Block sizes: 8" x 5" and 8" x 11". Quilt size: 45½" x 21½".

FROM JEAN'S DESIGN JOURNAL:

Fabric Selection

All of the fabrics in *Cushion Flowers* are batiks. Right off the bat, this creates a look that is different from conventional cottons. I started with a multicolored theme fabric for the border and extracted my color ideas from there. I look for similar tones rather than exact color matches. A quilt is less successful when everything matches up exactly.

The radiating stripes in the flower heads are created by intermixing different values and textures. In the middle flower, for example, there are medium values, dark values, textured batiks, solids, and near solids. These contrasts play up the radiating energy of the design. Rust circles accent each flower and pull them together as a group. For the background, I chose a much lighter version of one of the theme print hues. This lighter print keeps the mood elegant.

Quilting

Outline quilting and echo quilting were perfect for the simple leaf, stem, and background shapes in the lower portion of the quilt. The flowers are also outline-quilted. Anything more complicated would have competed with the colorful piecing. The quilting in the border mimics the design in the fabric.

M I N I   L E S S O N   *Making a Cushion Flower*

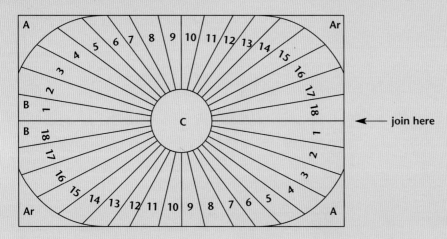

join here →

5. Place the A and Ar pieces on B, right sides together and matching the curved edges. Pin. With piece A or Ar (the concave edge) on top, stitch along the curve ¼" from the edge, using the point of a pin to keep the raw edges aligned. Stop and readjust the pieces as needed. On the wrong side, press toward A/Ar.

Cushion Flower blocks are pieced like Lazy Daisy blocks (page 74), except the corners are rounded off.

1. Paper-piece two B arcs in numbered order. Alternate the strip colors at random or in a repeated sequence for good color contrast. Trim the ends of the fabric strips even with the pattern.

2. Layer the B's right sides together, matching the C edges. Stitch together. Press.

3. Use the needleturn technique to appliqué C to the center of the block, concealing the area where the radial seams converge.

4. Using sharp scissors, make ⅛" clips every ¼" along the inside curved edge of A and Ar. Evenly spaced clips are essential for a smooth curved seam.

6. Press the completed block from the right side. Remove the paper pattern. Use a rotary cutter and ruler to true up the block to 8½" x 5½", for an 8" x 5" finished block size.

Materials

Use batik fabrics.

⅝ yard multicolor print (includes ¼ yard for binding)

½ yard light tan textured solid

½ yard deep green

¼ yard deep berry

⅛ yard rusty orange

⅛ yard each five to six coordinating colors

⅛ yard black textured solid

1½ yards backing

50" x 26" batting

Cutting

CUSHION FLOWER BLOCKS (5)

Use the patterns on page 80, enlarging as indicated. Prepare 10 B paper-piecing patterns. Prepare freezer paper patterns A, Ar, and C.

From the assorted fabrics except the light tan, the dark green, and the black, cut one 1¼" x 42" strip each for B. Cut additional strips during the paper piecing as needed.

From the light tan, cut 10 A and 10 Ar.

From the rusty orange, cut 5 C.

STEM BLOCKS (5)

Use the patterns on page 80, enlarging as indicated. Prepare freezer paper patterns D, Dr, E, Er, F, and Fr.

From the light tan, cut 5 D, 5 Dr, 5 F, and 5 Fr.

From the green, cut 5 E and 5 Er. Cut two 1½" x 42" strips. Cut into five 1½" x 11½" strips (G).

BORDERS

From the black, cut two 1¼" x 42" strips. Set aside one strip for the top inner border. Cut the other strip into two 1¼" x 5½" strips for piecing the side inner borders.

From the deep berry, cut two 1¼" x 42" strips. Set aside one strip for the bottom inner border. Cut the other strip into two 1¼" x 11½" strips for piecing the side inner borders.

From the multicolor print, cut three 2½" x 42" strips. Sew into one long strip. Cut into two 2½" x 18" strips for the side outer borders and two 2½" x 46" strips for the top and bottom outer borders.

Assembly

1. Refer to Making a Cushion Flower (page 78). Paper-piece 10 B's in sets of two, using three to four different fabrics per set. Make three dark sets, one medium set, and one light set. Stitch together in pairs. Press. Join the A's and Ar's at the corners. Press. Appliqué C to the center of each block. True up each block to 8" x 5" plus seam allowance.

Cushion Flower Block
Make 5 assorted

2. Stitch D to E. Press. Stitch E to F. Press. Make five total plus five more in mirror image. Join together in pairs, inserting G in between, to create five stems with leaves.

Stem Block
Make 5

3. Stitch the Cushion Flower blocks and Stem blocks together. Press. Lay side by side as follows: dark, medium, dark, light, dark. Stitch together in a row. Press.

4. Stitch the black and deep berry side inner border strips together. Press. Sew the strips to the sides of the quilt top as shown in the quilt photograph (page 77) and quilt diagram. Press. Add the top and bottom inner borders. Press. Add the side outer borders. Press. Add the top and bottom outer borders. Press.

5. Layer and quilt as desired.

QUILT DIAGRAM

Block Key

◻ Cushion Flower block
◻ Stem block

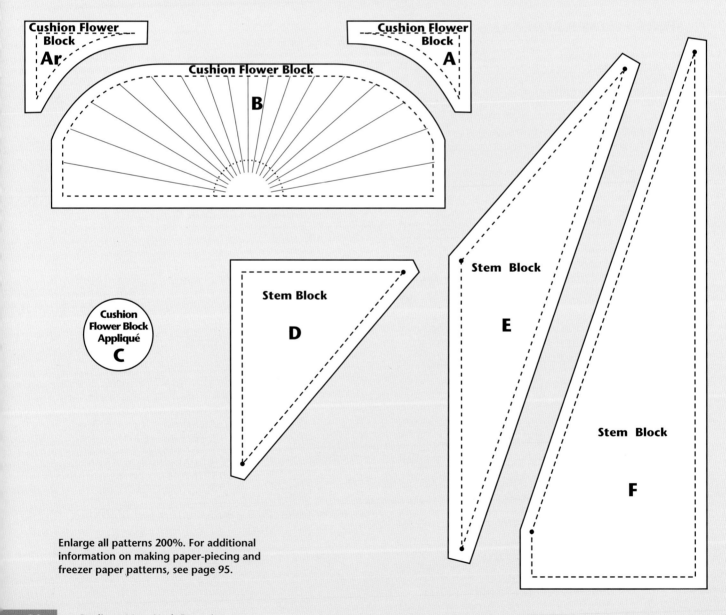

Cushion Flower Block **Ar**

Cushion Flower Block **A**

Cushion Flower Block **B**

Cushion Flower Block Appliqué **C**

Stem Block **D**

Stem Block **E**

Stem Block **F**

Enlarge all patterns 200%. For additional information on making paper-piecing and freezer paper patterns, see page 95.

Sorbet Sunrise

Early mornings in the garden inspired the colors and theme for *Sorbet Sunrise* by Jean Wells. The quilt uses three different blocks—Aria, Lazy Daisy, and Cushion Flower. Each Aria block has three paper-pieced arcs, giving the pattern more depth. The radiating designs in the blocks and careful color choices and placement work together to create this stunning visual treat. Block sizes: 15½" x 12½", 10" x 12", and 8" x 5". Quilt size: 41½" x 49½".

The Cushion Flower blocks running down the side of the quilt were the most fun to make. I experimented with different fabrics, mimicking the light-to-dark, top-to-bottom color progression set up in the rest of the quilt. I kept the colors random and scrappy for a playful look.

Easy Stitch 'n Flip piecing gave me the look of grass almost instantly. I looked for different colors and textures of green to create depth in the design. I love how orange accents the greens and purples and makes the design sing. Working with this summery garden palette in late December and early January was a treat.

Quilting

A few years ago, Valori encouraged me to try free-motion quilting. I have to admit I was scared that my stitches wouldn't be consistent. With her coaching, I found my own path. Today, I can hardly wait to get to the quilting.

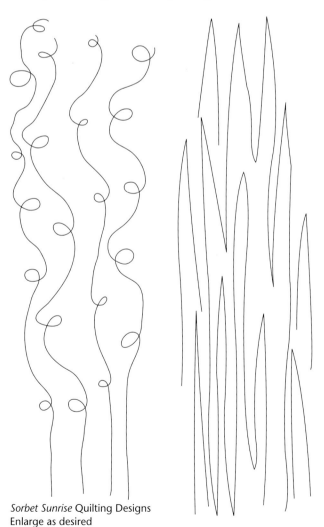

Sorbet Sunrise Quilting Designs
Enlarge as desired

FROM JEAN'S DESIGN JOURNAL:

Fabric Selection

I began this quilt wanting to capture the sunrise and those first yellow rays shining down on a pink and purple flower. I kept thinking about the colors and quality of light that I see when I am working in the garden in the early morning. The bright hues and dewy textures remind me of sorbet. Touches of green appear here and there.

My large purple flower contains four Aria blocks, but I wanted them to convey a single design. I asked Valori to change some of the plain arcs into pieced arcs to give me more pattern to play with. The colors transition from arc to arc, ending with purple on the outside points and peaches, pinks, and yellows toward the middle. For the very center, I found the perfect yellow and pink sunflower batik. I liked the movement it gave to the overall design. I feel like I am painting with fabric when I make these color decisions. I look until I find the very special tones that I want.

I chose richer, darker colors for the Lazy Daisy blocks. Deeper shades of purple and orange appear at the top of these off-center blocks, and greens mix in toward the bottom.

I see quilting lines as the icing on the cake. Here is where I can work in details to enhance the piecing. I follow my instincts when choosing quilting lines, looking for motifs that I can easily repeat. In *Sorbet Sunrise*, radiating lines come out from the sun, grass grows behind the flowers, and more grassy lines are stitched in alongside the pieced blocks. In the Lazy Daisy flowers, I quilted lines that end in curls, resembling tendrils or ferns about to unfurl their new growth. All of these lines are inspired by nature and help convey the essence of the quilt.

Stitch 'n Flip Blocks   MINI LESSON

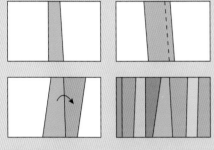

Stitch 'n Flip piecing has the look of complicated patchwork, but it's actually done on a muslin foundation. It's an especially fast, effective way to add color and design lines to background blocks and fillers.

1. Cut a piece of muslin ½" larger all around than the finished block. For example, if the finished block is 8" x 5", start with an 9" x 6" muslin rectangle. Cut strips of fabric in assorted widths and colors, depending on the look desired.

2. Place one strip right side up in the middle of the muslin. Trim the ends of the strip even with the edge of the muslin.

3. Place a contrasting strip on top of the first strip, right sides together and with one long edge aligned. Machine-stitch ¼" from the edge through all three layers.

4. Flip the second strip over the seam allowance. Finger-press from the right side. Trim the edges of the second strip even with the muslin.

5. Repeat steps 3 and 4, cutting some of the strips at a slight angle to skew the seams. Continue until the entire muslin foundation is filled. Press the finished block from the right side. Trim the block to the finished size plus a ¼" seam allowance all around. For an 8" x 5" block, trim to 8½" x 5½".

Materials

Use hand-dyed fabrics and batiks.

2½ yards total assorted greens and aquas (includes ¼ yard for binding)

½ yard total assorted dark greens (includes ⅛ yard for binding)

1⅓ yards total assorted pinks and peaches

1½ yards total assorted purples and violets

1 yard yellow

⅓ yard orange

1⅝ yards backing

⅝ yard muslin (for foundation piecing)

46" x 54" batting

Cutting

ARIA BLOCKS (6)

Enlarge the patterns on pages 58–59 250%. Enlarge the patterns on page 87 200%. Prepare 3 B, 3 Br, 3 CC, 3 CCr, 3 DD, and 3 DDr paper-piecing patterns. Prepare freezer paper patterns A, Ar, E, Er, F, and Fr.

From the yellow, cut 1 A, 1 Ar, and three 4" x 42" strips for the B/Br background.

From the assorted greens and aquas, cut 2 A, 2 Ar, and six 4" x 42" strips for the B/Br background.

From the assorted pinks and peaches, cut three 3½" x 42" strips for the B/Br points, two 2½" x 42" strips (emphasize pink) for the CC/CCr background, four 2" x 42" strips (emphasize peach) for the CC/CCr points, and three 2" x 42" strips for the DD/DDr background.

From the purples and violets, cut six 3½" x 42" strips for the B/Br points, three 2½" x 42" strips for the CC/CCr background, and five 1½" x 42" strips (two that emphasize violet, three that emphasize purple) for the DD/DDr points. Also cut 3 E and 3 Er (emphasize violet).

From the orange, cut two 2" x 30" strips for the DD/DDr background. Also cut 3 F and 3 Fr.

Sort the pieces by block, referring to the quilt photograph (page 81).

LAZY DAISY BLOCKS (3)

Use the patterns on page 76, enlarging as indicated. Prepare 3 A, 3 Ar, 3 B, and 3 Br paper-piecing patterns. Prepare freezer paper pattern C.

From the assorted purples, pinks, and greens, cut one 1⅝" x 42" strip each to start. Cut additional strips as needed during piecing. You will need the equivalent of five to six strips per block.

From a dark pink, cut 3 C.

CUSHION FLOWER BLOCKS (3)

Use the patterns on page 80, enlarging as indicated. Prepare 6 B paper-piecing patterns. Prepare freezer paper patterns A, Ar, and C.

From all the assorted fabrics except green, cut one 1¼" x 42" strip each for B. Cut additional strips as needed during paper-piecing. You will need the equivalent of five to six strips per block.

From the light greens and aquas, cut 6 A and 6 Ar.

From a dark pink, cut 3 C.

FILLER BLOCKS & SASHING

From the muslin, cut two 9" x 42" strips. Cut into one 9" x 2½" rectangle (A), three 9" x 5" rectangles (B), two 9" x 5½" rectangles (C), and two 9" x 7" rectangles (D). Also cut one 3½" x 38½" strip (E).

From the assorted greens, cut one 2"-wide strip each. Cut additional strips as needed during the foundation piecing.

From a dark green, cut two 2¼" x 12½" rectangles (F).

BINDING

From a light green, cut three 1¾" x 42" strips, or enough for 112" total.

From a dark green, cut two 1¾" x 42" strips, or enough for 65" total.

Assembly

1. Refer to Paper-Piecing an Arc (page 10) and Paper-Piecing Irregular Points (page 42). Paper-piece the following arcs: 3 B, 3 Br, 3 CC, 3 CCr, 3 DD, and 3 DDr. Try to vary the values from point to point and be playful with the color placement.

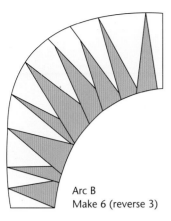

Arc B
Make 6 (reverse 3)

Arc CC
Make 6 (reverse 3)

Arc DD
Make 6 (reverse 3)

2. Refer to Joining Curved Sections (page 11). Join A to B, matching the background colors. Join an AB unit, CC, DD, Er, and Fr to make three Aria blocks. Join Ar, Br, CCr, DDr, E, and F to make three Aria reverse blocks.

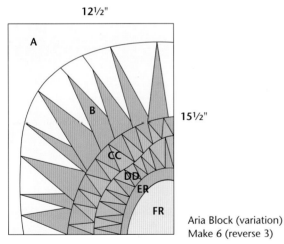

12½"

15½"

Aria Block (variation)
Make 6 (reverse 3)

3. Refer to the *Lazy Daisy* quilt instructions, steps 1–4 (page 74). Paper-piece the following Lazy Daisy units: 3 A, 3 Ar, 3 B, and 3 Br. Use purples and pinks for the A's and Ar's. Use mostly dark greens for the B's and Br's, but work in a few light green, pink, and purple accents as shown in the quilt photograph (page 81). Stitch the units together in AB and ArBr pairs. Press. Join the pairs to make three blocks. Appliqué C to each block to conceal the seam intersection.

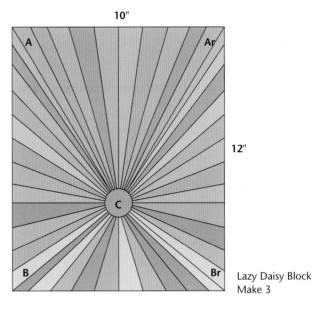

10"

12"

Lazy Daisy Block
Make 3

4. Refer to Making a Cushion Flower (page 78). Paper-piece 6 B's in sets of two. Make the first set pink, orange, and yellow, the second set orange, pink, and purple, and the third set purple and violet. Stitch together in pairs. Press. Add an A or Ar to each corner. Press. True up each block to 8" x 5" plus seam allowance. Appliqué C to the center of each block.

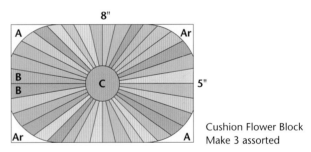

8"

5"

Cushion Flower Block
Make 3 assorted

5. Refer to Stitch 'n Flip Blocks (page 83). Use the stitch 'n flip technique to fill muslin rectangles A through D. Use lighter greens for A, B, and C and darker greens for D, angling the seams to suggest grass. Intersperse a few light purples and pinks among the greens as you piece. Make eight pieces total. Trim A to 8½" x 2", B to 8½" x 4½", C to 8½" x 5", and D to 8½" x 6½".

6. Use the stitch 'n flip technique and 4"- to 7"-long green and aqua strips to fill muslin strip E. Start at one end, sewing a few green and aqua strips at an angle across the width of the muslin strip. Let some of the raw edges land on the muslin. To hide them, lay the next strip at an angle. Stitch 'n flip. Now you have a new direction in which to fill. When the new section is filled to capacity, lay down a new strip and change the direction again. Continue in this way, interspersing a few pinks, purples and darker greens, as shown in the quilt photograph (page 81), until the entire strip is filled. Trim to 3" x 38".

7. Lay out all the pieces as shown in the quilt photograph and quilt diagram. Stitch the Cushion Flower and filler blocks A, B, C, and D in a column, pressing after each addition. Stitch the

Aria blocks together in rows. Press. Join the rows. Press. Add E to the right edge. Press. Stitch the Lazy Daisy blocks together in a row, inserting sashing strips in between. Press. Join these three units, pressing after each addition.

8. Layer and quilt as desired. Use the light and dark green binding strips to create the two-color binding shown in the quilt photograph.

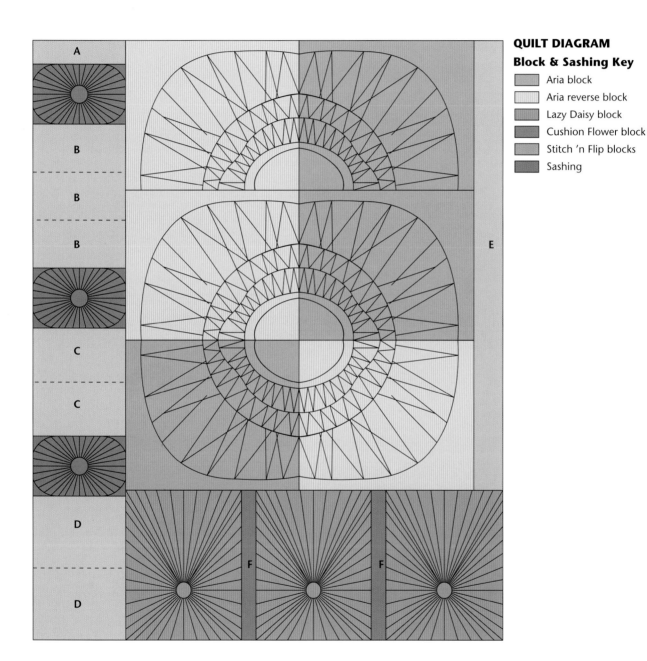

QUILT DIAGRAM
Block & Sashing Key

- Aria block
- Aria reverse block
- Lazy Daisy block
- Cushion Flower block
- Stitch 'n Flip blocks
- Sashing

Enlarge all patterns 200%. For additional information on making paper-piecing and freezer paper patterns, see page 95.

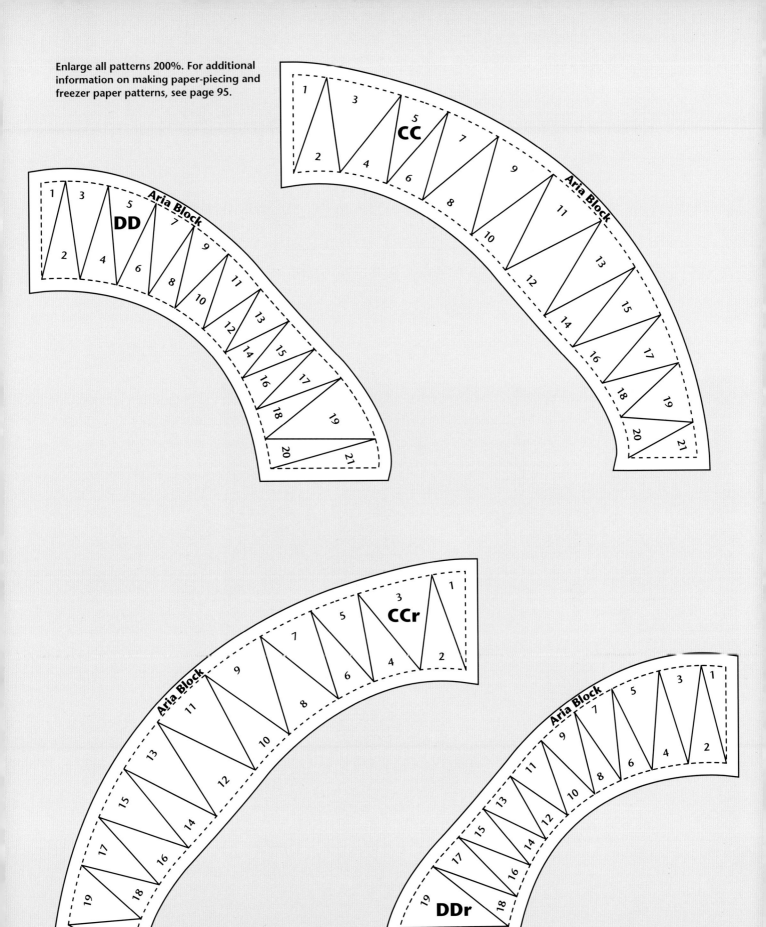

Starburst

When I created *Starburst*, I was imagining the garden at night, the flowers exploding with color—if only we could see them through the darkness. The blocks in this quilt are not that difficult to sew. It is what to do in the negative space that is the challenge and also what makes the quilting fun. The design lends itself to so many possibilities in color choices and quilting. Block size: 7" x 7". Quilt size: 57" x 50".

Fabric Selection

For our 2001 employee quilt challenge, we chose a brand-new collection of batiks that I had designed. When I studied these fabrics with the challenge in mind, I wanted to add black. Instinct told me the colors would appear brighter and even more brilliant against a black ground. Black fabric makes them glow.

I drafted the block so that the points were narrow and explosive. Then I started grouping colors and making blocks, using black for the background throughout. This quilt was different for me because I didn't plan it out. I didn't even make a sketch. I just kept making blocks and grouping them together to build the design.

Even though the colors came from a single collection, it was a challenge to make them all work together in the quilt. How the colors are placed affects how your eye moves around the quilt. It occurred to me as I worked how completely different the design would come across made up in another palette. Instead of stark black, the plain squares could be cut from a theme print and the New York Beauty colors pulled from it. The filler blocks between the pieced blocks offer a ready canvas for lots of color and fabric possibilities.

Quilting

Starburst was a blast to quilt. I really wanted the stitching to be visible within the dark empty spaces, so I chose brightly colored thread. I found a flower with pointy petals and a large circular center to use as my model. Rather than quilt the same design over and over again, I placed tracing paper over the blank areas of the quilt top and drew each flower individually. By elongating the petals beyond the block seam lines, I was able to fit each flower to its space. Each one came out a little different. Tracing out the design helps me get acquainted with it and puts it into my memory. When it comes time to actually quilt, I'm already in gear. Even when I use free-motion quilting, I still like to sketch the design on the quilt top with a chalk pencil. I don't always follow the lines exactly; they act more as a guide.

The starbursts in the New York Beauty blocks are quilted with matching thread. The stitching lines in the center circles are curved in some blocks, pointed in others. The arc points are so narrow, I just ran the thread up and down each one. Small curlicues extend from the starbursts, as if they are giving off little sparks of color into the night.

The border quilting was something I hadn't thought about at all, which is unusual for me. I stared at the border for a long time and finally decided the quilting needed to be simple. The result is a thorny stem that runs all around and relates visually to the pointy quilted flowers and starbursts.

Starburst Quilting Design
Enlarge as desired

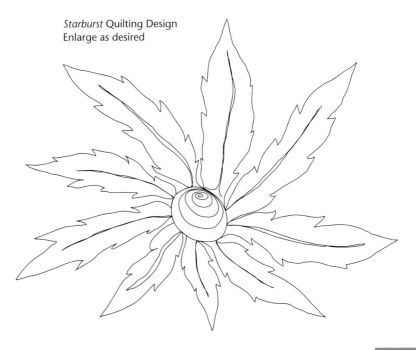

Materials

5 yards black (includes ⅜ yard for binding)

1 yard multicolored batik

½ yard each pink, yellow, violet, and turquoise

⅜ yard each blue, gold, and purple

¼ yard each olive green, light green, and brown

⅛ yard each rust and coral

3 yards backing

61" x 54" batting

Cutting

The black border strips for this quilt can be cut on the lengthwise grain to avoid excessive piecing. If you choose this option, cut the border strips first, before you cut the block pieces, and adjust the B strip length as necessary.

BLOCKS (42)

Use the patterns on page 91, enlarging as indicated. Prepare 33 B paper-piecing patterns. Prepare freezer paper patterns A and C.

From the black, cut nine 7½" squares, 33 A, and twenty-seven 2½" x 42" strips for B.

Cut all the colored batiks (except the multicolored piece) into ⅛-yard cuts, for 33 assorted 4½" x 42" pieces. From each piece, cut 1 C. Cut the remainder into one 2" x 38" strip and one 2½" x 38" strip for B. Sort the pieces by color.

BORDERS

From the multicolored batik, cut six 2½" x 42" strips. Sew into one long strip. Cut into two 2½" x 55" strips for the side inner borders and two 2½" x 62" strips for the top and bottom inner borders.

From the black, cut six 2½" x 42" strips. Sew into one long strip. Cut into two 2½" x 55" strips for the side outer borders and two 2½" x 62" strips for top and bottom outer borders. Set aside the remaining black for the binding.

Assembly

1. Refer to Paper-Piecing an Arc (page 10) and Paper-Piecing Irregular Points (page 42). Using one colored fabric per arc, make 33 B arcs with colored points and black backgrounds.

2. Refer to Joining Curved Sections (page 11). Sew A, B, and C together, matching the colors of the B points and C. Make 33 blocks total.

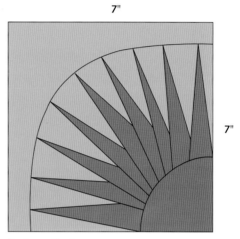

Starburst Block
Make 33

3. Lay out the Starburst blocks and black squares in six rows of seven blocks each. Rotate the pieced blocks to compose full and partial starbursts in various colors, as shown in the quilt photograph (page 88) and quilt diagram. Stitch the blocks together in rows. Press. Join the rows. Press.

4. Sew the inner and outer border strips together in black/multicolored pairs. Press. Refer to Making Mitered Corners (page 37) to attach and complete the borders. The multicolored strips form the inner border in this design.

5. Layer and quilt as desired.

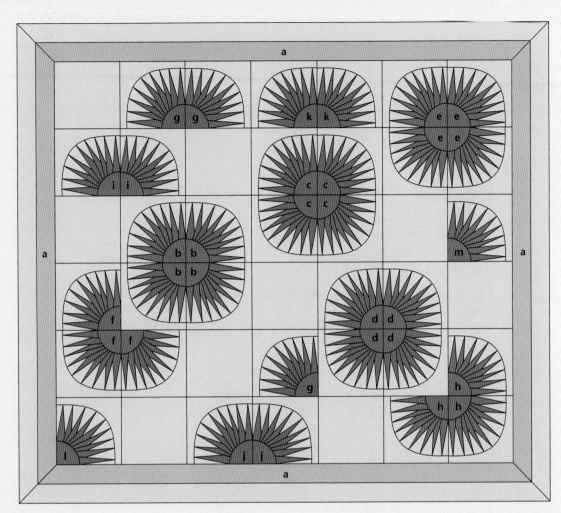

QUILT DIAGRAM
Fabric Key

a   multicolor
b   pink
c   yellow
d   violet
e   turquoise
f   blue
g   gold
h   purple
i   olive green
j   light green
k   brown
l   rust
m   coral

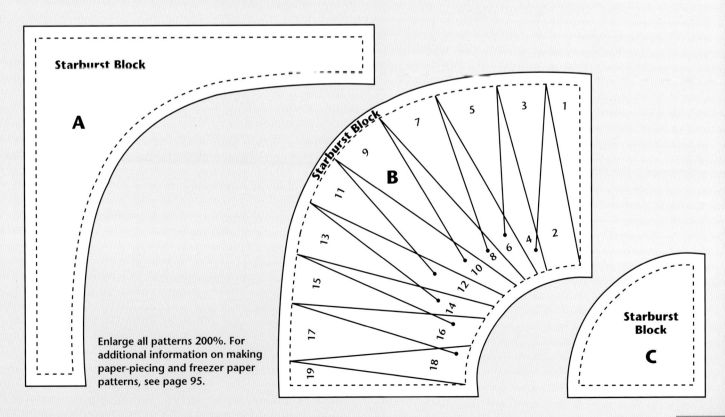

Starburst Block

A

Starburst Block

B

7 5 3 1

9

11

13

8 6 4 2

10

12

15

14

17

16

19

18

Enlarge all patterns 200%. For additional information on making paper-piecing and freezer paper patterns, see page 95.

Starburst Block

C

Joshua Tree
A Quilter's Journal

Joshua Tree, designed by Valori Wells. Block size: 8" x 8". Quilt size: 57" x 50".

I was in Palm Springs one winter and borrowed a car from a friend to go explore Joshua Tree National Park. With my camera and sketchbook in hand, I started through the park. I spent most of the day on the dirt jeep roads, seeing the trees and rocks in a non-tourist setting.

I found the Joshua trees especially interesting. Before this trip, I had only seen them in photos, never in person. The shape, texture, and personality of the trees are unique. I liked how the

This page: Photographs and sketches from my trip to Joshua Tree National Park.

young trees were just one stock but the mature trees had multiple limbs that seemed to sprout randomly from the main trunk. The way the greenery grew out of the tree limbs, radiating sharp, pointy leaves, made me think of New York Beauty blocks.

When I returned home and developed my photographs, the trees and rock formations intrigued me even more. The contrast between the rounded rocks and the pointy Joshua tree inspired me to draft my quilt. I wanted to capture the tree against its natural setting of rock outcroppings.

I had already drafted the Starburst block. I decided that it would be perfect for this quilt. I reduced the block size and then added piecing into the center to intensify the pointy shapes. Since my blocks were already a specific size, I drafted the rest of the quilt to match. I drew in rock formations, the tree trunk and branches, and sky, knowing I could use freezer paper templates later on to subdivide these blocks for piecing. Once the foundation of the quilt was determined, I went to the fabric.

Hand-dyed and hand-painted fabrics give this quilt a natural look. Using my photographs as a color reference, I selected different grays, browns, and off-whites to create depth in the rocks. Once the background fabric was determined and the New York Beauty blocks were made, I turned my attention to the quilt assembly. I started at the top

This page: Taking photographs of the quilt as I go helps me evaluate the design from a different perspective.

each block before moving to the next, to gradually build the quilt.

Once the top was done, I determined that it needed a border. A single color just didn't seem to work around the whole quilt, so I looked back to my photographs for inspiration. I thought I might try piecing a border from different fabrics to match the edge of the quilt all around, only a value or two deeper. I used dark brown at the bottom and up to where the rocks ended and transitioned to deep blue where the sky began. By choosing colors in the same family as the quilt, I achieved a framed effect without interrupting the flow of the picture. The border is wider on two edges. I am not sure why, but the quilt just seemed better balanced to me this way.

At this stage, the quilt was humming along. I was counting on the final touch—quilting—to make it sing. Once again I consulted my photographs, looking for ways to enhance the dimensional quality in the rocks. Simple lines of stitching helped me create these soft contours in the rocks, in contrast to the pointy lines in the Joshua tree. The entire quilt was such a treat to make. I love the process of taking photographs, making sketches, and interpreting them in a quilt.

of the quilt, cutting out the fabric and placing it on the design wall. When I reached a block that required two fabrics, I cut a freezer paper square the same size, drew the required contours on it, and cut the paper block apart to make individual templates. I then pressed each template onto the correct fabric with a warm iron, cut ¼" beyond the edge for the seam allowance, and sewed the pieces together. I proceeded in this way, piecing

Making and Using the Patterns

MAKING ENLARGEMENTS

The block patterns in this book must be enlarged 200% on a photocopier, unless noted otherwise. The quilting designs can be enlarged to any desired size. Depending on the size of copier paper available, you may have to copy the pattern in sections and then tape the sections together. Use a light box or place the sheets up against a window to line up the pattern lines. Apply small pieces of Scotch tape to the unlined areas of the pattern only. Try to avoid taping directly over the stitching lines. If you do stitch through tape, replace the needle and clean the throat plate and bobbin mechanism of your machine.

PAPER-PIECING PATTERNS

Paper-piecing patterns are used to make arcs with points. Each arc is stitched from the wrong side, and the pattern is the reverse of the final shape. You will need to make one paper-piecing pattern for every arc you sew. I recommend photocopying the pattern onto a lightweight paper sold in quilt shops especially for this purpose. The lighter-weight paper tears away more easily than regular copier paper after the stitching is complete. You can also trace patterns by hand onto tracing paper, but this takes much longer.

FREEZER PAPER PATTERNS

Freezer paper patterns are used to cut the plain sections in the New York Beauty block. Freezer paper is sold in most grocery stores and in some quilt shops. It has a wax coating on one side that adheres to the fabric when pressed with an iron. These self-adhering patterns are amazingly accurate and easy to use.

Tear off a sheet of freezer paper and place it shiny side down on the printed pattern. Trace the pattern outline on the dull side of the freezer paper, using a ruler to draft straight lines accurately. Cut out the pattern on the marked line.

The patterns in this book already include the seam allowance.

Place the pattern wax side down on the wrong side of the fabric. Press with a dry iron on the cotton setting, moving the iron up and down until the pattern adheres to the fabric. Cut around the edges, using a rotary cutter and ruler for straight edges and sharp scissors for the curves. Peel off the paper when you are ready to sew. You may reuse the patterns several times.

Freezer paper is also used to make appliqué templates. An appliqué template does not include a seam allowance and is pressed to the right side of the fabric. For more details, see page 20.

DRAFTING ARC PATTERNS

To draft arc patterns, use sheets of graph paper, either eight-squares-to-the-inch or four-squares-to-the-inch, in a size larger than the desired block dimensions. To draw curves, use a flexible curve ruler or a compass. The flexible curve ruler can be shaped any way you like and lets you add an accurate one-quarter-inch seam allowance as well. A compass lets you draft traditional arcs up to a certain size; for larger arcs, try the rim of a big bowl or some other creative substitution. An 18-inch C-Thru ruler marked with a grid is handy to use. For thin, accurate lines, try a mechanical pencil.

QUILTING DESIGNS

The quilting patterns in this book can be used in two ways: as sources of inspiration or as actual stitching patterns. To use a pattern for stitching, enlarge it and then trace it on a large sheet of tracing paper. When you trace the design with a pencil, you are actually memorizing the contours and the path the line takes. Pin the tracing to the layered quilt, stitch on the design lines through all the quilt layers, and then tear the tracing away. After awhile, you will find that you will be able to stitch designs freehand without a tracing pattern to guide you.

About the Author

Valori Wells draws her inspiration from nature, using photography to capture the images and scenes she wants to re-create in quilting and fabric design. A designer at heart, she sees ideas and is able to capture them in her artistic endeavors.

A graduate of Pacific Northwest College of Art, Valori received the school's "Outstanding Photographer of the Year" award in 1997. Since then, she has become involved in the family store, The Stitchin' Post, in Sisters, Oregon, where she uses her talents in pattern and book design and is involved in the daily tasks of running a business.

In Spring 2002, she participated in the Sisters High School "Painted Strings" benefit to promote the study of traditional folk music. Valori decorated a guitar with black-and-white photos of peonies and made a fabric case quilted with peonies to go with it. Her work generated the highest bid at the charity auction. Valori has collaborated with her mother, Jean Wells, on several books that combine gardening and quilting themes, and she is the solo author of *Stitch 'n Flip*. This talented young woman designs fabric for Free Spirit.

Index

Sources

For additional inspiration, try Karen K. Stone's *New York Beauty* paper-piecing patterns ($18) and *New York Beauty* border pattern supplement ($12). Both available from:

New York Beauties
Karen K. Stone
5418 McCommas Blvd.
Dallas, TX 75206-5626
karen@karenkstone.com
www.karenkstone.com

For fabrics & quilting supplies:

The Stitchin' Post
P.O. Box 280
311 West Cascade
Sisters, OR 97759
541-549-6061
www.stitchinpost.com
Call or write for a mail order catalog or visit the website.

Cotton Patch Mail Order
3405 Hall Lane, Dept. CTB
Lafayette, CA 94595
800-835-4418
quiltusa@yahoo.com
www.quiltusa.com

RMS SEGWUN
QUEEN OF MUSKOKA

∽ Andrew Hind & Maria Da Silva ∽

DUNDURN
TORONTO

Editor: Allison Hirst
Design: Courtney Horner
Printer: Transcontinental

Library and Archives Canada Cataloguing in Publication

Hind, Andrew
    RMS Segwun : queen of Muskoka / Andrew Hind and
Maria Da Silva.

Includes bibliographical references and index.
Issued also in electronic formats.
ISBN 978-1-4597-0442-8

    1. Segwun (Steamboat). 2. Mail steamers--Ontario--
Muskoka--History. 3. Steamboats--Ontario--Muskoka--
History. 4. Muskoka (Ont.)--History. I. Da Silva, Maria
II. Title.

VM627.O5H56 2012   386'.50971316   C2011-908014-1

1 2 3 4 5   16 15 14 13 12

  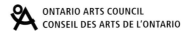

We acknowledge the support of the **Canada Council for the Arts** and the **Ontario Arts Council** for our publishing program. We also acknowledge the financial support of the **Government of Canada** through the **Canada Book Fund** and **Livres Canada Books**, and the **Government of Ontario** through the **Ontario Book Publishing Tax Credit** and the **Ontario Media Development Corporation**.

Printed and bound in Canada.
www.dundurn.com

Dundurn
3 Church Street, Suite 500
Toronto, Ontario, Canada
M5E 1M2

Gazelle Book Services Limited
White Cross Mills
High Town, Lancaster, England
LA1 4XS

Dundurn
2250 Military Road
Tonawanda, NY
U.S.A. 14150

CONTENTS

The *Segwun* stops alongside an area boathouse in a scene that evokes the essence of Muskoka.
Courtesy Muskoka Steamships.

FOREWORD

A crowd gathers on the dock as it becomes apparent the captain is getting ready to accept passengers. You can sense the anticipation as the crew welcome everyone aboard and people young and old make their way to a spot on the bow or to a table in the dining room, awaiting departure. At the top of the hour the Segwun pulls away from the wharf with a single the blast of her whistle; arms wave and cameras flash. The captain welcomes everyone with a personal message as the ship slowly turns in Gravenhurst Bay; another Segwun cruise has begun.

You would think that watching this scenario play out more than a thousand times over the past ten years would dull the experience — it doesn't. The words "just another day at the office" are never spoken around here, and each day brings with it hundreds of enthusiastic people ready to embark on a journey filled with fun, romance, and history. Some sail with us every year, some have cottaged in Muskoka for years but are onboard for the first time. Whatever the occasion, *Segwun* never disappoints. Sailing aboard her is truly a magical Muskoka experience that is not to be missed.

Segwun will celebrate her 125th anniversary in 2012, a milestone in the history of Muskoka. She is the oldest Royal Mail Ship in the world, the oldest commercial vessel in Canada, and the seventh oldest steamship in the world. Quite the resume! But none of it would have been possible without the vision of a dedicated group of volunteers who championed *Segwun*'s 1981 restoration despite heavy criticism. Almost a million passengers later, *Segwun* has become a tourism icon and been the catalyst for other projects, such as *Wanda III*, *Wenonah II*, the Muskoka Boat and Heritage Centre, and the Muskoka Wharf. With the continued support of the people of Muskoka and passengers from across the globe, *Segwun* will continue to make her historic trips through the scenic lakes of Muskoka.

Andrew and Maria have embraced *Segwun* since they took their first cruise aboard her in 2009. Their story begins with the first steamship, *Wenonah*, and carries the reader through the years to the present day, with detailed narratives and colourful tales about the ships and people of the Muskoka Lakes Navigation Company.

This book is a wonderful tribute to RMS *Segwun* on her 125th anniversary, so please enjoy — and don't forget to book your passage, today!

John Miller
General Manager
Muskoka Steamship and Historical Society

Most of the *Segwun*'s cruises are relatively short jaunts out onto Lake Muskoka, but she also occasionally passes through the locks at Port Carling into Lake Rosseau, a great thrill for spectators watching from shore.
Courtesy Muskoka Steamships.

ACKNOWLEDGEMENTS

The authors are enormously indebted to a great many institutions and persons who very kindly supplied us with priceless information, personal memories, and other forms of assistance. In particular, they wish to acknowledge the assistance of the following people: John Miller, general manager of Muskoka Steamships, who kindly agreed to write the foreword for the book; the entire staff and crew of Muskoka Steamships for allowing us unrivalled access to *Segwun*; Mary Storey and Ann Curley of the Muskoka Boat and Heritage Centre for invaluable assistance, in particular with sourcing photographs; Jim Caldwell, former captain of *Segwun*; Jon Massey, sales manager, and the staff at Residence Inn by Marriott, Muskoka Wharf; Ruth Holtz of the Bracebridge Public Library; Stephen Elliott and James Hind for providing cartographical help; and Ron Sclater.

Special attention should also be drawn to all the volunteers, past and present, who helped build the exhibits and collections of the Muskoka Boat and Heritage Centre; without their unheralded efforts over the years, our job of researching this book would have been much more difficult.

A Note from Andrew Hind

Despite having spent 38 years cottaging in Muskoka, until Maria and I took our first cruise aboard *Segwun* in 2009, I was unfamiliar with the historic ship's fascinating story and her timeless appeal. Since then, and most particularly during the course of writing this book, I've learned to appreciate *Segwun* as the treasure she is. As a result, I want to thank Maria for encouraging that first experience aboard the Queen of Muskoka and for accompanying me on the voyage that led to the publication of this book. She is the best friend one could hope for.

I also want to thank Barry Penhale at Dundurn for his support of this book from the very beginning. It's greatly appreciated.

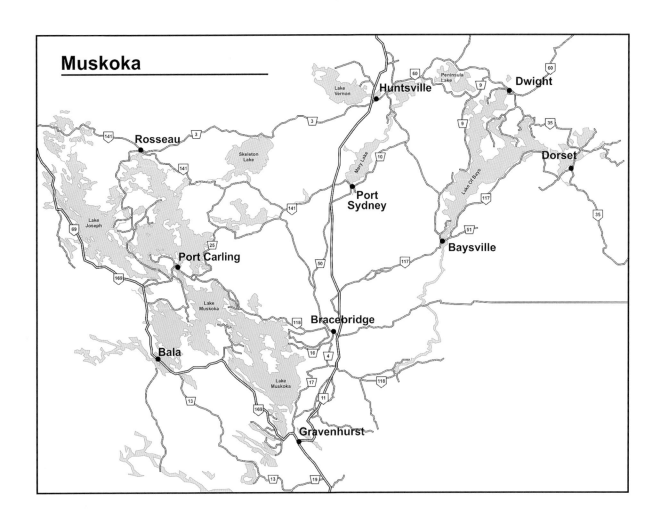

INTRODUCTION

At the time of writing, the Royal Mail Ship *Segwun* is celebrating her 125th anniversary, and she has seen a lot over those years. When she was built in 1887, as *Nipissing II*, she was just one of many steamships plying the lakes and rivers across Ontario. But today she is the last of her kind, a vestige of a bygone era and a beloved Muskoka icon and popular tourist attraction.

Departing from the Muskoka Wharf in Gravenhurst, *Segwun's* route takes her through Lakes Muskoka and Rosseau, with the occasional jaunt out onto Lake Joseph. The scenery is impressive there at any time of day — a shore lined with windswept pines and magnificent homes and cottages. But the views take on a whole new magnificence as the sun starts to dip below the horizon. As a result, even though *Segwun* had many different cruises available, that first time aboard we chose the sunset dinner cruise. We were not disappointed.

Our first glimpse of the ship was memorable. Smoke was spewing from the stack as the steam engine warmed up, and we couldn't believe how beautifully *Segwun* had been restored. Although more than a century old, the ship did not appear to have aged, and stepping aboard was like travelling back in time.

We presented our tickets to the purser, crossed the gangplank, and ducked our heads as we passed through into the wooden hull. Directed upstairs, we passed by the engine room, where we heard loud scraping noises coming up from the bowels of the ship — the distinct sound of coal being shovelled into the boiler.

Climbing the same stairs that countless feet had trod up in the past, we found our way to the Islander Restaurant, located at the bow, and one of two dining areas onboard. As we sat at our table, we could tell that *Segwun* was preparing to pull away from the dock by the distinct vibration of the engines underfoot. And although we feared the motion of the water might get the better of us, once underway, it was like being in any other dining room.

The setting was divine. Not only did we take in the spectacular vistas as we sailed along at a leisurely pace of six knots, but it was quite easy for us to imagine the passengers who would have taken a similar cruise a century before. No land-based restaurant could compete with this combination of scenery and nostalgia.

An hour later, and our meals finished, we were anxious to head up on deck to watch the sunset. That's part of the experience, after all. And it *was* breathtaking. The hum of the engines, heard and felt several decks above, only added to the enjoyment, soothing and relaxing us as we gazed out on the beauty of Lake Muskoka.

While on deck, we met a group of about 15 college-aged students who had decided to take the cruise, many for the first time. They had friends visiting from Australia who wanted a "touristy" experience. It was nice to see members of the younger generation enjoying the cruise and the history of the area. It warmed our hearts despite the chilly breeze rolling in off the water.

A part of this history was shared with us when we climbed up to the wheelhouse to chat with the ship's skipper. Captain Jim Caldwell, who retired in 2010, was a veteran sailor, a man perhaps more comfortable with the subtle roll of waves underfoot than on dry land. After 29 years aboard ships plying the Great Lakes, Caldwell had served on *Segwun* for a further 21 years. "I've had a lot of great times and met people from all over the world," the captain told us, a faraway look in his eyes. "And this ship, with its history, is hard to leave."

While spinning the ship's wheel, Captain Caldwell told us tales of *Segwun's* past and related some of his memories of his time aboard her. We eagerly soaked it all in, and it was at that time that we conceived the idea for this book; we felt strongly that the stories he regaled us with that night should be shared by all.

When we finally descended from the wheelhouse and wandered into the cozy lounge, we met Kate Cox, who had been working as a bartender on *Segwun* for 14 years. She served us with a mile-wide smile, the fabulous beverages she brought us warming our chilled bodies. For the rest of the cruise she kept us entertained with stories about the ship and the people who had been aboard, crew and passengers alike. Some stories were hilarious, and some touched the heart strings, but all were entertaining.

Kate spoke about the vessel with obvious affection. "Everyone loves this ship," she told us. "It seems magical somehow." During her years aboard, Kate had met numerous celebrities on the ship, including Goldie Hawn and Kurt Russell, and soap opera star Lisa Rinna and her husband, actor Harry Hamlin. Maria also learned that her favourite actor, Nicolas Cage, once filmed a movie on the ship.

But it's the common people who Kate remembered the most, the people like her who fell under the enchantment of *Segwun*. "People from all over the world love this ship because [they feel as if] they're going back in time. It's the nostalgia. There's nothing more romantic, more memorable, than a sunset dinner cruise aboard the *Segwun*," she told us. "There's something magical about the ship. Can you believe that in all my years aboard, it has never rained during a wedding? It might have rained in the morning or been overcast, but it has never rained during the ceremony. It's almost like the ship is blessed."

Author Maria Da Silva was captivated by her first cruise aboard *Segwun* as described in the text.
Courtesy of Andrew Hind and Maria Da Silva.

There is something special about a cruise aboard *Segwun*. There's an authenticity in the way her coal-fired steam engines can be felt through the deck plating; in the sound of her whistle, the beating heart of Muskoka can be distinctly heard.

As the ship slowly docked alongside the wharf, we found ourselves overwhelmed by the experience — the spectacular views of the lakes, the great food, and the wonderfully hospitable crew. And we discovered a new appreciation for the *Segwun* itself. This historic vessel that has been sailing on the Muskoka Lakes for more than a century had a rich story to tell, and it's a story we were honoured to write.

Today, Muskoka Steamships operates a second vessel alongside *Segwun* — the modern *Wenonah II* — that combines all the style of a 1907 Muskoka steamship with the latest conveniences. Although she dwarfs *Segwun* in size, we believe that newer and bigger doesn't always mean better. *Segwun*, despite her age and more intimate stature, remains a unique vessel, and one that links us to the history of this region.

So let's step aboard this historic steamship and slip back in time to find out why she is so cherished.

A Note About Names

The RMS *Segwun* has gone by two names during her lengthy history; she began in 1887 as *Nipissing II* but was renamed *Segwun* after an extensive rebuild in 1925. Throughout the text, we refer to the ship as it was known in the historic period being discussed. The Muskoka Navigation Company has also gone by a number of names, all of them relatively subtle variations. To avoid confusion, we refer to it as the Muskoka Lakes Navigation Company throughout.

CHAPTER ONE

Laying the Foundations of Muskoka Steamboating

The RMS *Segwun* was the product of a revolutionary technology, the steam engine, which brought about the most visible change in ship design in centuries. The steam revolution started in the 1780s with the first efforts to propel a ship using steam power, and the first successful steamboats appearing in the first decade of the 19th century. William Symington built the *Charlotte Dundas* in Scotland in 1802, while in the United States, Robert Fulton's *North River Steam Boat* hit the waters in 1807. The use of maritime steam engines grew quickly; it was clearly a revolutionary step forward, since the use of the new technology freed ships from their reliance on the wind. The first generation of steamships used paddlewheel propulsion, and then came the breakthrough of the screw propeller, which came into use in the 1830s. From that point on, steam-driven ships began to slowly but steadily supplant sailing vessels.

This evolution occurred in Ontario as elsewhere in the Western world. Steamboats followed settlers and lumbermen into the back lakes and rivers; as civilization moved northward, it brought with it its steamships. Indeed, some would argue it was the steamships that brought civilization to those remote areas. In many regions, whole industries and communities were dependent on steamers for moving both people and commodities. Even after the railways appeared in the 1850s, steamships remained a vital form of transportation. In fact, far from competing, steamships and trains, for the most part, complemented each other.

When the first settlers began trickling across the Severn River and into the frontier of Muskoka in the early 1860s, there was no reliable form of transportation beyond the few rutted, rock- and stump-strewn roads that passed through the oppressive forests. In a region dominated by lakes and rivers, waterways were clearly the best route for transporting people and goods. The area's Native people had long known this, and it was obvious to even casual observers. But someone would have to step forward with the drive and ambition to put a steamship on the Muskoka Lakes. That person was Alexander Peter Cockburn.

In 1866, A.P. Cockburn, a visionary entrepreneur, took his first trip to Muskoka. He liked what he saw in the untamed but resource-rich region, and expressed his enthusiasm for the area in conversations with Darcy McGee, the minister of agriculture in the Ontario government at the time. Cockburn offered to put a steamer on the lakes to encourage settlement if the government would agree to build a lock at Port Carling (to link Lake Muskoka and Lake Rosseau) and a canal at Port Sandfield (linking Lake Rosseau and Lake Joseph). This would enable continuous navigation between the three bodies of water. In fact, Cockburn was so convinced of the future possibilities for the area that he went ahead with the launching of his steamboat, *Wenonah*, in 1866, without receiving definite assurances from government officials that they would actually move forward with these infrastructure projects.

Wenonah, an 80-foot sidewheeler, was a far cry from the refined style of later steamships. Furnishings

No known images of the original *Wenonah* exist. However, this vessel, also owned by A.P. Cockburn, inherited that vessel's steam engines, her name, and much of her appearance. Unlike the first *Wenonah*, this ship operated on the Magnetawan River.
Courtesy of Muskoka Boat and Heritage Centre.

were spartan, her engines were noisy and capable of only a modest eight miles per hour, and passengers were forced to travel on the upper deck, where they were at the mercy of the elements. Even so, *Wenonah* proved a real godsend to the region's early settlers. It offered a vital link between communities separated by many miles of bush and greatly reduced travel times. Vast quantities of freight and mail were also transported by water, offering a better alternate to the rutted, primitive roads of the day. As well, *Wenonah* towed logs by the hundreds to area sawmills.

But despite the obvious benefits to settlers and businessmen, the steamship failed to earn a profit for its owner for several years. Worse, she frequently grounded on rocks and shoals in the uncharted waterways. Many men would have despaired and given up after those first frustrating seasons, but not Cockburn. He persevered, and when the steamship finally began to turn a profit in 1868, he must have felt a great sense of satisfaction.

The success of *Wenonah* only made the continued dithering of the government in regard to the proposed lock and canal more frustrating and inexplicable. So Cockburn was forced to take matters into his own hands, and he submitted a petition to the Legislature that called for a lock at Port Carling. The petition had been signed by hundreds of Muskoka residents, and it finally prodded the government into action. John Carling, the commissioner of public works, was sent to look at the sites and to report back about the feasibility of the lock and canal. Cockburn acted as host, sharing with the commissioner his vision of a profitable navigation system opening up the country. His enthusiasm obviously rubbed off on Carling, who submitted a favourable report, and work on the lock began the following year.

As they were breaking ground on the lock project, Cockburn launched a second ship, *Waubamik*, to join *Wenonah* on the lakes. It was a bit of a gamble, as *Wenonah* was only just making money, but Cockburn felt he had to maintain his monopoly on shipping in the area. The government was offering inducements to entrepreneurs to put a steamboat on Lake Rosseau, and Cockburn was certain that if he didn't jump on the opportunity, someone else undoubtedly would. Besides, having two boats had obvious advantages: one could carry freight and passengers, while the other could be used to tow logs; and if one ship were damaged, there would be another to pick up the slack.

Passengers wait to board *Nipissing II* at a private dock on Keewaydin Island, located on Lake Muskoka.
Courtesy of Muskoka Boat and Heritage Centre.

By 1871, Cockburn recognized that even two ships weren't sufficient to service all the communities on both lakes, and so he ordered the construction of a third steamer. The new ship was built in Gravenhurst and was modelled after a famously graceful Lake Simcoe steamer, the *Emily May* — though it would be one-sixth the size, so that it would fit through the locks at Port Carling.[1] With a price tag of $20,000, she was the most impressive vessel Cockburn had built. A double-decked paddlewheeler measuring 115 feet long by 19 feet wide, she grossed 150 tons and could attain a speed of 14 miles per hour. Cockburn chose to name her *Nipissing*, an Ojibwa word meaning "little body of water."

The *Nipissing* served as the flagship for Cockburn's fleet. Admired by the crew for her fine qualities, she was equally beloved by passengers for her beauty and smooth sailing. Meals were served in her finely outfitted salon, where sparkling glasses and spotless white table linens gave the impression of elegance. If there was one complaint, it was that *Nipissing* lacked a hurricane deck, which meant that passengers were exposed to the elements and exhaust from the ship's stack. That oversight in her design was rectified in 1877 when *Nipissing* was put in dry dock and overhauled.

Having founded the navigation company and finally persuaded the government to build the lock, Cockburn turned his attention to bringing the railway to Muskoka. The Toronto, Simcoe and Muskoka Junction Railway issued a charter in 1869 to build a railway line from Barrie to Gravenhurst, but lack of funds saw the project stagnate. The tracks had reached the town of Orillia by 1872, but there they stopped. The Severn River and the rock of the Canadian Shield formed an obstacle to further construction, and for a time it looked as if this was as far as the line would ever go. Cockburn would not be deterred, however, and kept the project alive with his enthusiasm and passion. He talked at length to railway officials, investors, and government representatives, stressing the need for the railway and all the benefits it would bring: markets for settlers, rapid shipment for merchants, a whole new watershed full of untapped timber for lumber companies — and an influx of tourists. Finally, in part due to Cockburn's insistence, work on the rail line resumed in 1875, and that fall, the train rolled into Gravenhurst for the first time.

The arrival of the railway and the resulting boom in industry and commerce, particularly tourism, greatly benefitted Cockburn's steamship line. All three vessels were hard at work, rarely at less than full capacity in terms of passengers, cargo, or towed logs. During the 1870s, *Nipissing* most often sailed on Lake Muskoka, connecting with *Wenonah* at Port Carling. Later, as the fleet expanded and more steamers were built, she generally ran from Gravenhurst to Rosseau (three times a week) and from Gravenhurst to Port Cockburn, at the head of Lake Joseph (on alternate days).

In many ways, a sailor's life in the 1870s was much the same as it had been for centuries. The captain and his mate stood at the wheel and piloted the vessel, porters loaded cargo, and ropes were coiled by deckhands. However, steam propulsion had created a new category of mariner — the men who fed and ran the steam engines. This divided the crew into two categories — the deck sailors, who filled the traditional roles of sailors, and the "black gang," who ran the engines. The black gang consisted of coal-heavers (easily the least skilled but most physically taxing position), whose responsibility it was to feed the furnace with coal, and firemen, who tended the boilers and watched the engines under the supervision of an engineer.

Engine rooms were dangerous places, even when everything was working properly: a slip could result in burns from contact with the hot machinery; heat exhaustion and dehydration were ever-present threats; equipment failure — whether through wear, bad construction, or damage — could allow scalding steam to escape; and, most devastating, steam engines always ran the risk of sparking a fire that could claim the entire ship. In fact, the latter brought about the destruction of *Nipissing* in 1886.

It was at Port Cockburn where the majestic steamship met her untimely demise. On the night of August 3, while at anchor, a fire broke out in *Nipissing*'s engine room. By the time the crew caught the scent of smoke, jumped from their bunks, and raced to investigate, the blaze was already burning out of control. There was nothing they could do to save the ship, and with the flames spreading rapidly they focused on saving themselves. To their horror, the crew found the gangways a raging inferno. With flames closing in, and choking smoke making it increasingly difficult to breathe, several crewmen climbed through windows and jumped overboard, most wearing nothing but their nightshirts. Worried that the fire would spread to the docks and beyond, the steamer was cut loose and left to drift to a nearby island, where she burned to the waterline and sank. Divers claim that the skeleton of the old *Nipissing* is still visible in the depths just off Fraser Island.

The loss of *Nipissing* was a devastating blow to the company. But no sooner had the ship sunk beneath the waves than the unflappable A.P. Cockburn began to formulate plans for her successor.

CHAPTER TWO

ALEXANDER COCKBURN

The Muskoka many of us know and love today — a land of carefree summer vacations and fond memories — owes much to the founder of the Muskoka Lakes Navigation Company, Alexander Peter Cockburn. Without his vision and persistence, there would likely have been a much different story to tell. Cockburn's contributions did not go unnoticed, and in 1900 a writer at the *Huntsville Forester* referred to him as "The Father of Muskoka Tourism."

Alexander Peter Cockburn was born on April 7, 1837, in the village of Berwick, Finch Township, Stormont County, Upper Canada (now Ontario). His parents, Peter Cockburn and Mary McMillan, were prominent figures in the young community, hard-working and enterprising individuals who passed on these traits to their three sons. Alexander's father was predominantly involved with the lumber trade, harvesting and milling trees. It was a prosperous business at that time, and he ensured his son had a good education and encouraged him to explore outlets for his developing ambitions. One of these ambitions was politics, and as a teenager Alexander helped a local Reformer, Samuel Alt, get elected. Early lessons learned about the manner in which politics worked would serve him extremely well in the years ahead.

By the 1850s, Berwick no longer seemed big enough for Peter Cockburn. He craved new horizons to explore, and besides, the supply of harvestable trees in the area was all but exhausted. So he decided to pull up stakes and move his family to the village of Kirkfield, east of Lake Simcoe, and go into business for himself as a general merchant. The move paid off handsomely, and once again the family prospered, becoming prominent figures in Eldon Township. Alexander assisted his father for a number of years, but by 1863 his ambitions could no longer be contained, and the 26-year-old opened his own store and became the village postmaster. A year later, he was elected reeve of Eldon. He was re-elected in 1865, and narrowly missed becoming county warden, as well.

Even as Alexander was finding success in business and politics, personal happiness came his way, and on September 24, 1864, he married Mary Helen Proctor of Beaverton, whose father was the leading industrialist in Thorah Township. Together they would raise five daughters and a son.

The year 1865 represented a turning point in Cockburn's life. In the fall of that year he visited the Muskoka District, which was at the time was only just being opened up for settlement. It was intended primarily as a recreational trip with friends — three weeks spent canoeing the waterways that weaved across the region — but it's likely that he was also eyeing future opportunities. Cockburn was delighted with Muskoka's natural beauty, and came away from the experience certain that the district had great potential for settlers and lumbermen, as well as for sportsmen, for whom the establishment of wilderness resorts would soon follow. During that three-week period was born a passion that would see A.P. Cockburn become Muskoka's greatest champion.

After publishing a pamphlet extolling the potential of the area, in the spring of 1866 Cockburn returned to Muskoka, settling in Gravenhurst. That year, he built a large store in town, established the first stage service connecting with the steamer terminus at Washago, and opened a sawmill at Musquash Falls in Bala. Most important, as far as his legacy was concerned, he also launched the first steamboat on Lake Muskoka — *Wenonah* — which he was even known to take command of on occasion.

Cockburn remained passionately interested in politics, and throughout his lengthy career he used his platform as a means of promoting Muskoka. In 1867, Cockburn, running as a Liberal, was elected by a large majority as member of provincial parliament for Victoria North, an area that included Muskoka. He was instrumental in persuading the government of John Sandfield Macdonald to survey several additional northern townships and to pass the Free Grants and Homestead Act of 1868, both of which were vital to the settlement of Muskoka. Late in 1867, Cockburn initiated the founding of the Muskoka Settlers' Association, of which he was predictably elected president.

By the spring of 1869, Cockburn had convinced the Ontario government to build a lock on the Indian River at Port Carling and a canal at Port Sandfield that would allow steamers to extend their runs to Lakes Rosseau and Joseph. He also pressed to have the Northern Railway extended from Barrie to Gravenhurst, so that, by the fall of 1875, Muskoka had a direct link to Toronto and beyond. This led to a boom in lumbering and tourism in the region. His popularity soared as a result of the regional improvements he helped bring about, and in 1872 Cockburn easily defeated D'Arcy Boulton for the federal seat of Muskoka. He was re-elected in 1874, and again four years later.

Cockburn had a flair for promotion, and during his lifetime he wrote dozens of pamphlets that colourfully described the region's natural splendour, the rejuvenating qualities of its clear waters and fresh air, and the bounty of fish and wildlife that made the region a sportsman's paradise. He widely promoted Muskoka and wrote so vividly of its appeal that people clamoured to visit. It was his vivid descriptions that inspired William H. Pratt of New York to open a resort hotel — the Rosseau House ("Pratt's Hotel") — on Lake Rosseau in 1870. Its success prompted others to open resorts in the area, and Muskoka was well on its way to becoming a popular tourist destination.

By 1905, the Muskoka Lakes Navigation Company was at the peak of its success, enjoying a profitable and exciting time that seemed to validate Cockburn's faith in the value of the steamboat. That year the line had eight steamers in operation (soon to be nine with the launch of *Sagamo*). They catered largely to the 60 or so lakeside resorts (a figure up from 30 around the turn of the century), which had combined accommodations for around 5,000 visitors. Indeed, the most palatial of these resorts, the Royal Muskoka, was owned by the company, and served as a shining beacon of the optimism sweeping the region. Tourism in Muskoka had truly arrived and the Muskoka Lakes Navigation Company was reaping the financial benefits.

Alexander Peter Cockburn, the "Father of Muskoka," photographed in 1879 during his time as a Member of Parliament.

Courtesy of Muskoka Boat and Heritage Centre.

19

Unfortunately, A.P. Cockburn, whose life mission it had been to guide and nurture Muskoka to this moment, did not live long enough to boast of his success and foresight. Though he had experienced recurring heart problems since being laid low by a serious bout of influenza in 1891, on June 2, 1905, he seemed in good health and vibrant spirits. That evening, however, his wife noticed Cockburn had grown pale and was having trouble breathing. Alarmed, she sent for a doctor, but before help could arrive, Cockburn died of a massive heart attack. He was 68 years old, and left his wife and five children to mourn his passing.

Cockburn had not enjoyed any great financial windfall from the success of the company he had founded; rarely drawing a wage, he once described himself as "one of the hardest worked and worst paid transportation managers upon the continent."

A.P. Cockburn's riches lay in the legacy he left behind. The *Muskoka Herald* published a fitting tribute, noting that with Cockburn's death, "Muskoka loses one of its best friends, one who, believing in its possibilities, invested his money here when the District was a wilderness and who, conscientiously, in parliament and out of it, sought to advance its best interests…. He was well and favourably known throughout the entire District and his death will be regretted by many friends."[1]

Flags aboard the navigation company's steamships were flown at half mast for a week following his death. A special train arrived in Toronto on the day of his funeral bearing hundreds of Muskoka's leading citizens, each of whom respected Cockburn for his tireless devotion to the region's development, which, over the course of 40 years, had been instrumental in transforming the region from a trackless wilderness frontier into North America's premier tourist destination. His steamships had, as he had predicted they would, encouraged settlement in the region and stimulated the growth of industry and commerce.

For very good reason, Alexander Peter Cockburn has been known ever since as the Father of Muskoka.

CHAPTER THREE

NIPISSING II

I mmediately after *Nipissing* was lost, A.P. Cockburn began making plans for a replacement. The demand for shipping on the Muskoka Lakes dictated that he have at least three large steamers operating at any given time, so the decision was based very much on necessity and the realities of his growing business. To cut down on costs, the new steamship would inherit the engine and boilers salvaged from the charred remains of *Nipissing*. The new ship would also inherit its predecessor's name: she would be christened *Nipissing II*.

Beyond shared engines and name, the two vessels had a great deal else in common. They were, for example, nearly the same size, with an overall length of 128 feet, a beam of 21 feet (excluding the distinctive paddle boxes), a gross tonnage of 275, and drawing about six feet of water. They looked almost identical, as well, so much so that it's often difficult for modern observers to tell them apart in photographs. However, close

A spectacular image of *Nipissing II* in 1893. The ship was later renamed *Segwun*.
Courtesy of Muskoka Boat and Heritage Centre.

examination does reveal a few differences: The *Nipissing II* had a noticeably shorter smokestack, and both her paddle boxes and pilothouse were styled differently. One particularly distinguishing feature of *Nipissing II* was the carved wooden phoenix mounted on the wheelhouse. Crafted by the ship's skipper, Captain George Bailey,[1] it was a highly symbolic ornamentation: like the mythical bird that had risen from the ashes, so, too, had *Nipissing* been reborn out of fire — better and more beautiful than ever.

The most important difference between the two ships was the method used in the construction of their hulls. Whereas the original ship was built of locally harvested wood, *Nipissing II*, up to the main deck, was constructed

Spectators look on as *Kenozha* pulls in behind *Nipissing II*.
Courtesy of Muskoka Boat and Heritage Centre.

Nipissing served many of Muskoka's finest summer hotels, including Beaumaris, pictured here.
Courtesy of Muskoka Boat and Heritage Centre.

of Welsh iron. She was manufactured at the Clyde Shipyard of Davidson and Doran in Scotland, with the hull sections being shipped across to Toronto, and then on to Muskoka Wharf by rail. There they were assembled and riveted, the machinery installed, and the wooden superstructure added. When she was launched in the spring of 1888, *Nipissing II* became the first iron-hulled steamer to sail on any of Ontario's inland waterways.

Passengers loved the vessel for her graceful appearance and smooth sailing. Officers appreciated her manoeuvrability and rapid rate of acceleration and reverse, and she was easily the fastest steamer in the fleet. The one drawback, her crew would reluctantly admit, was that in open water, when facing a stiff headwind, she found herself at a disadvantage compared to her screw-driven sisters because the paddles "couldn't get good purchase."

Cockburn loved *Nipissing II* because she was an efficient vessel, routinely carrying as many as 300 passengers at a time and more cargo than any of her sister ships. Like her predecessor, the new steamer served as the flagship of the company fleet and would retain this honour for 15 years, only relinquishing it when the larger, more modern *Medora* entered service in 1902.

Initially, *Nipissing II* served almost exclusively on the Lake Joseph run, leaving Port Cockburn at either 6:30 or 7:30 a.m. and meeting the incoming train at Muskoka Wharf at 12:25 p.m. Within an hour she would be fully loaded and setting sail for Beaumaris, Port Carling, Ferndale, Minett, Port Sandfield, Redwood, Hamills Point, and YoHo Island. She would return to Port Cockburn around 7:00 p.m. Twelve hours later her crew would be back aboard and the ship would depart to repeat the process. In 1893, the new steamer *Muskoka* took over the route, and *Nipissing II* assumed the Rosseau run, which involved her serving the various resorts and communities located along the shores of that lake.

George Bailey was a masterful mariner, but he had his share of misadventure while commanding *Nipissing II*. Once, while sailing down the length of Lake Muskoka toward Gravenhurst, a heavy fog descended without warning — one minute the lake was clear and visibility was good, and the next a dense, grey cloak had settled over the water and trapped the ship in its cold embrace. Visibility was reduced to no more than a few feet, and Captain Bailey signalled down to the engine room to reduce speed to dead slow. *Nipissing II* cautiously crept forward. Handing the wheel to another officer, Captain Bailey went out on deck to appraise the situation. Concern was etched on his face; there was simply no way to safely navigate. Bailey's eyes grew wide as dark shadows suddenly loomed out of the fog directly ahead. He immediately called for full reverse. Unfortunately, it was too late, and the ship grounded on the rocks, tree branches sweeping the forward deck.

Nipissing II had run aground on Old Woman Island, near Walker's Point. Bailey ordered the crew to reverse engines, but the ship was stuck firm, and there she sat until another vessel arrived to drag her off. While no real damage had been done, Captain Bailey was humiliated by the mishap and had every intention of resigning his command. A.P. Cockburn, however, knew the accident wasn't the captain's fault, and, knowing that he had little hope of finding a replacement with Bailey's vast experience, he persuaded the old sailor to stay on.

In 1900, after 13 years on the water, *Nipissing II* was put in dry dock for much-needed repairs and some major renovations. Her paddlewheels were lowered to get better traction in the water and the paddle boxes were rebuilt. The pilot house was moved from the promenade deck to the top of the bridge, which was extended forward to provide a platform to accommodate it. The space below, formerly the old pilothouse and a cabin, was transformed into a handsome new ladies' lounge. The dining room at the stern was also enlarged. Once completed, the ship could carry as many as 400 passengers, and once back in service, did so regularly. With these improvements, the old paddlewheeler was well-equipped to sail into the 20th century.

Just four years after the costly reconstruction, *Nipissing II* was nearly lost. On the evening of July 7, 1904, she was cruising past Juddhaven on her way to Rosseau when wisps of smoke were seen coiling out from the forward lounge beneath the bridge. When members of the crew investigated, they found the room thick with smoke, and they watched with horror as flames suddenly erupted. Panic swept through the 40 passengers aboard. The crew sprang into action, fighting the fire with hoses and pails of water. It wasn't long before the fire was contained, but the episode showed how quickly a pleasant cruise could turn disastrous. An investigation showed that the fire had started when someone dropped a match or cigar down behind a cushion on a settee built around the stack.

After *Sagamo* joined the fleet in 1906, *Nipissing II* was given lighter duties to reduce the stress on her aging engines. She began running a subordinate route along the east side of Lake Muskoka, departing daily at 8:45 a.m. from Point Kaye to visit Port Keewaydin and the resorts around Milford Bay, then on to Beaumaris and Gravenhurst, returning by 6:30 p.m. Though the route was perhaps less glamorous than those previously run, it was still an important part of the company's efforts to provide service to all the ports and resorts on the lakes.

Despite efforts to nurse her engines, however, it wasn't long before the inherited machinery began to fail. On August 24, 1908, she ran into trouble between St. Elmo and Beaumaris when her piston suddenly exploded, blasting a hole in the hurricane deck above and damaging other machinery. No one was injured, but *Nipissing II* was stranded in the middle of the lake and had to be towed back to the wharf for lengthy repairs. The troubles persisted, and in 1912 the steamer was again pulled out of service for a few weeks when a shaft broke. On another occasion, the head of the steam cylinder blew off in mid-lake, allowing scalding steam to spew out, leaving her completely disabled. The crew could do nothing but blow the whistle for help and drop anchor to avoid drifting into the shore.

Despite these setbacks, the graceful sidewheeler continued on. However, the end was near at hand, the final straw coming in the summer of 1916. *Nipissing II* was being backed out of Milford Bay on Lake Muskoka when the main shaft on the walking beam broke, immobilizing her machinery. The disabled ship began to drift toward the nearby rocks. Hearing her persistent whistle calls, a boy named Francis Fowler came out to investigate in a small four-horsepower boat. The passengers, aware that something was wrong, leaned over the railing to watch with some amusement as Fowler's tiny boat began pushing the stern of the ship away from the rocks. The youngster took the steamer in tow and began to pull her toward Beaumaris at a speed of about three miles an hour. Eventually, another ship, the *Islander*, turned up to collect the passengers and tow *Nipissing II* the rest of the way into port.

With the First World War well underway at the time, spare parts were hard to obtain, and the old *Nipissing II* was left to languish at the company dockyards for the next few years. From time to time she was used as sleeping quarters by yard crew and other employees of the company, but otherwise she sat empty and ignored. As the years passed and decay set in, it began to look as if *Nipissing II*'s sailing days were over. Few could have known that, far from being over, a new and exciting chapter in the ship's story was about to be written.

CHAPTER FOUR

GETTING THERE WAS
HALF THE FUN

For many, it has become an annual tradition: when the hot summer days arrive and we feel the need to escape the heat, we make the scenic drive to the northern country. Whether we head to the cottage or to a vintage resort, we're compelled to find a place with lush woods and crystal-clear water. But do any of us really stop to think how this tradition began? Do we think about how our ancestors escaped the heat and humidity in an era with no air conditioning, a time when one couldn't simply hop into an automobile to flee the city?

A.P. Cockburn saw the appeal of Muskoka as a summer tourist destination and understood that easy access was the key to promoting the region. During the 1860s, his stage and steamer services were critical in opening the Muskoka frontier, and in the 1870s, thanks in part to his hard work and political influence, the Grand Trunk Railway extended its tracks to Gravenhurst. These developments — the founding of the Muskoka Lakes Navigation Company and the arrival of railways — allowed the tradition of escaping to the north to enjoy some fun in the sun to begin. The two modes of transportation complemented each other, and for many the journey by rail and steamer was a beloved part of the vacation experience.

Bear in mind that most people didn't just visit the area for a weekend or even a week; many would remain for the entire summer. Families had to bring along anything they might need during their stay. Large steamer trunks held many of these necessities, but vacationing families were even known to bring along dairy cows for fresh milk, chickens for eggs, and their horses. This was especially true of the early cottagers, rather than those summering at a resort. The sheer amount of luggage brought would be difficult for us to imagine today.

So with trunks full, the journey started. Regardless of where they called home — the United States, other areas of Ontario — vacationers would board the Muskoka Express train at Union Station in Toronto to embark on their first step northward. Hundreds of eager vacationers would pack the platforms —women trying desperately to keep cool in their long dresses and multiple layers, while keeping a watchful eye on children chasing one another around. The men, meanwhile, would perhaps light up a cigar, leaf through a newspaper, or strike up casual conversations with one another. Then, above the din, the station master would call out "Muskoka Express!" and the crowd would make their way toward the hissing train. Soon after, the engine would pull out, a trail of smoke behind, the wilds of Muskoka ahead.

Travellers aboard the Muskoka Express would have been quickly put at ease by the soothing sounds and vibrations of the train. Passing through the miles and miles of rolling hills and scenic farmland of central Ontario, the stress and heat of the city would be slowly left behind. Some passengers would be lulled to sleep by the motion of train, while others would keep their faces pressed to the window glass or talk with nearby passengers. The trip from Toronto to Gravenhurst was approximately 176 kilometres, so the express wouldn't pull into Muskoka Wharf until well after dark. From there, passengers would transfer to a steamer; but since the ship wouldn't leave until the next morning, they would spend the night in the passenger cars.

The next morning, Muskoka Wharf would be chaotic as the vacationers disembarked the express and prepared to board the steamers, docked nearby. As they waited to board the ship, many people forged what would become long-lasting friendships. The kids got to play a bit of hide and seek around the massive trunks, women exchanged pleasantries, and the men shared a cigar or two. These conversations would often bring families together, and sometimes future holidays with new friends were planned.

Passengers transferred from train to steamships at Muskoka Wharf in Gravenhurst. Men and women of the era dressed up for all occasions, including the journey north to their vacation destinations.
Courtesy of Muskoka Boat and Heritage Centre.

While the travellers mingled with one another, all those heavy trunks had to be moved from the express to the steamer, a task that must surely have been backbreaking for the porters who raced to complete the work as quickly as possible. Often they would start the transfer well before dawn, while the passengers were still asleep. It was hard work, but at least it meant that the porters' pockets were being filled with hefty tips — compensation for nursing sore backs during the busy season.

But the company was all about providing outstanding service: from the lowly deckhands, who wheeled tons of coal into the stoke-hold in the wee hours before dawn, to the waitresses who took

Above: Passengers enjoyed full breakfasts and lunches in the dining room aboard *Segwun*. This attention to detail contributed to a memorable vacation experience.
Courtesy of Muskoka Boat and Heritage Centre.

Left: A menu from the Muskoka Lakes Line, *circa* 1930.
Courtesy of Muskoka Boat and Heritage Centre.

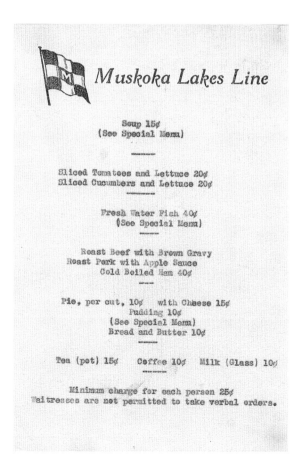

Muskoka Lakes Line

Soup 15¢
(See Special Menu)

Sliced Tomatoes and Lettuce 20¢
Sliced Cucumbers and Lettuce 20¢

Fresh Water Fish 40¢
(See Special Menu)

Roast Beef with Brown Gravy
Roast Pork with Apple Sauce
Cold Boiled Ham 40¢

Pie, per cut, 10¢   with Cheese 15¢
Pudding 10¢
(See Special Menu)
Bread and Butter 10¢

Tea (pot) 15¢   Coffee 10¢   Milk (Glass) 10¢

Minimum charge for each person 25¢
Waitresses are not permitted to take verbal orders.

orders for breakfast and lunch. From the steward on up to the captain of the ship, all crew members had a role in making sure that the voyage on the steamer was enjoyable, ensuring that guests would return the following summer and for many summers thereafter. Their jobs, and the very success of the company, depended on it.

Finally, as the time of departure neared, the passengers would be directed aboard. The purser would meet them at the gangplank, check their tickets, wish everyone a pleasant cruise, and direct them up the stairs to the upper deck lounge.

From the pilothouse railing high above, like a monarch looking out upon his kingdom, the captain would keep watch, dressed in his navy blue uniform. When he was satisfied that all the passengers and cargo had been loaded, the gangplank would be hauled aboard and the heavy ropes cast off. Then, with a blast of her whistle, the vessel would back majestically away from the wharf.

Soon a bell would sound and passengers would make their way down to the wood-panelled dining room, where several waitresses would take breakfast orders. A hearty breakfast might include bacon and eggs, toast, cereal, juice, and coffee; the passengers at the time were generally quite wealthy and expected the best.

Their meals finished, most people would return to the upper decks to enjoy the remainder of their time aboard. If their destination was nearby, it may have only been an hour's journey, but for others the trip may have taken an entire day. No matter. With the sun shining above and the refreshing maritime breezes, it would have been an enjoyable experience. There were deck chairs in which to read a newspaper

Muskoka Wharf Train Station

The railway arrived at Muskoka Wharf in 1875, and a simple rectangular wood-frame building, the Muskoka Wharf Station, was built. The building burned down in 1895, paving the way for a more impressive structure. At that time, the wharf was a bustling place in the summer with all manner of land- and water-based transportation converging there – horse-drawn carts and buggies, steamships, private yachts, and steam-driven trains. Wealthy families, many with domestic servants in tow, would disembark from the trains and board the waiting steamboats or private launches, which would carry them to one of the many resorts and cottages on the lakes. Clearly, something more elaborate than the former shed was in order.

The second Muskoka Wharf Station was built in 1895. Of wood construction with gingerbread trim along the eaves, it was a two-storey rectangular building with a long veranda. The exterior of the upper level was built in the Tudor style with stucco and wood cross-sections. The interior had a waiting room, ticket office, and gift shop. Adjacent to the train station, there was a long roofed walkway to protect passengers and goods from the elements. This attractive and commodious station was far more appropriate for a place frequented by the upper tiers of society.

This second station served its function for more than 50 years, until the demise of the steamship era. It was dismantled in 1956.

or magazine, or passengers could chose to stand by the railing and watch as the ruggedly beautiful scenery slid by.

Things haven't changed all that much since that time. People still want to escape the oppressive summer heat of the city, and heading north to cottage country continues to be the preferred option for many. Enjoying a leisurely cruise aboard *Segwun* or her sister ship, *Wenonah II*, remains a highlight of the season for many.

What has changed, however, is the journey *to* Muskoka. Travelling today is much easier thanks to improved highways and faster automobiles, meaning the trip takes only a fraction of the time and is far less stressful. But one might ask: in our race for getting there quicker, have we lost something along the way? After all, in days gone by, getting to Muskoka was half the fun!

CHAPTER FIVE

MUSKOKA WHARF: THEN AND NOW

Gravenhurst's fortunes have always been linked to its waterfront. The history of the town and its wharf marched in step, with developments in one always affecting the other.

When first constructed, the rickety wharves built by settler James McCabe[1] along the shores of Muskoka Bay served as a stepping-off point into the wilds of Muskoka. Hotels, taverns, stores, and the shipping companies began to cater to this slow but steady trickle of homesteaders, and the town of Gravenhurst developed alongside the Muskoka Road, which led to the bay. It should, therefore, come as little surprise that Gravenhurst was originally known as McCabe's Landing. The name was changed in 1862 when the community was given a post office. (An official in the Post Office Department chose the name after seeing it in a book he was reading.)

The community grew steadily in the ensuing years, serving as the main port on the Muskoka Lakes and a terminus for the small but growing number of steamships plying their trade upon the pristine waters. Docks sprung up along Muskoka Bay to service the ships, each one crowded with immigrants eager to take up land provided free by a government determined to develop the region.

Activity along the wharf reached a fever pitch once the railway tracks reached Gravenhurst in August of 1875. On September 28, the first rail car hissed and steamed its way into town. Two months later, a spur line down to the lakeshore was built. There, in a sheltered cove a quarter-mile west of the Gravenhurst town wharf, the railway built Muskoka Wharf. The shoreline of Muskoka Bay was artificially extended with massive cribwork and fill to form a true wharf within the sheltered inlet. A waiting room was built and given the grandiose title of Muskoka Wharf Station, and trains would pull right up along the docks to disgorge their freight and passengers almost directly onto the steamships.

An early view of Muskoka Wharf in Gravenhurst, showing none of the refinement and boisterous activity that would later characterize the waterfront.
Courtesy of Muskoka Boat and Heritage Centre.

The Express arrives at the Grand Trunk Railway station at Muskoka Wharf.
Courtesy of Muskoka Boat and Heritage Centre.

The wharf was a boon to industry and settlement in the region. Hundreds, if not thousands of settlers passed through every year for almost two decades, and were joined by an equal number of summer tourists. Just as important were the vast quantities of goods that were shipped out: in 1878 alone, some 2,811 tons were loaded onto steamships from the wharf.[2]

The extensive wharves with rail access meant that lumber could be easily shipped to the wood-desperate markets of the American east coast. Geography played a role in Gravenhurst developing into a lumber town. Indeed, it's been said that Gravenhurst seemed to have been designed by nature to be a lumber centre. The bay is surrounded on the south and west sides by almost level ground, upon which thousands of board feet of lumber could be stockpiled before it was shipped out by train. In addition, the bay is sheltered from high winds and is spacious enough to accommodate tens of thousands of logs bobbing in the water. (Captain Levi Fraser estimated that at times it held as much as 50 million feet of lumber.)[3] Finally, and perhaps most importantly, the Lake Muskoka watershed ensured a seemingly endless bounty of forests to be harvested. Each spring, logs harvested from all over Muskoka, as well as parts of the Haliburton and Parry Sound districts, would be floated down rivers flooded by snowmelt, and into Lake Muskoka, ready to be towed to nearby sawmills.

With its rail access and geographic advantages, Gravenhurst became the location of choice for logging companies to establish sawmills, and they began to spring up like trilliums along the shores of Muskoka Bay. By 1883, there were 14 mills on the bay, and in that year alone 30 million feet of lumber, 35 million shingles, and 50 million feet of logs left Gravenhurst by rail.[4] It was said that the bay was so full of logs you could walk across it without getting your feet wet. During the period between 1875 and 1890, before railways finally pushed on to centres farther north, almost all of Muskoka's felled timber ended up in Muskoka Bay to be processed for shipping. For good reason, the town became known as "Sawdust City."

Largely spurred on by the lumber boom, Gravenhurst's population rose quickly during this era. From a few hundred lonely souls in 1875, it had swelled to 1,200 people by 1878 and 2,454 by 1887. Over half of the population worked at the mills. Most of the rest earned their living in businesses dependant on the lumber industry — hotels, taverns, and stores — or as craftsmen, brewers, or distillers.

The not-so-picturesque sawmills that once covered the area. Stumps in the foreground attest to the deforestation that was taking place at the time.
Courtesy of Muskoka Boat and Heritage Centre.

As a result of this frenzied sawmill activity, tourists arriving at Muskoka Wharf would have been greeted by a sight far different from the attractive vistas and pleasant, park-like setting of today. The bay would have been ringed by more than a dozen ramshackle and noisy sawmills, each one spitting smoke into the air and debris into the water. The landscape at the time was barren wasteland of rocks and stumps, the forests having been denuded of trees to feed the insatiable hunger of the saws. Muskoka Bay was clogged with logs, and vast piles of sawdust lined the shores like rotting mountains. Everywhere one looked there were rundown boathouses, docks, storage sheds, and discarded machinery or lumber.

The unsightly environs did little to discourage tourists from flocking to the region every summer, however. By 1900, up to five express trains a day were arriving at Muskoka Wharf, each one packed with excited vacationers looking forward to spending weeks, or often the entire season, at one of the dozens of resorts lining the shores of the Muskoka Lakes. The wharf was thriving, and at the time most residents of Gravenhurst would undoubtedly have looked to the future with unbridled enthusiasm, certain that the communal prosperity they were enjoying would remain indefinitely. Sadly, that was not to be the case.

Muskoka Wharf remained a hive of activity and industry for another couple of decades, but things collapsed rapidly in the 1930s. The decline of Muskoka Wharf wasn't attributable to one single thing, but rather a series of changes that combined to undermine the town's relevance. First, the region's supply of merchantable pine was all but exhausted by the end of the second decade of the 20th century, and even the big softwood sawmills ringing the bay were fast being silenced. As the lumber industry fell on hard times, so, too, did Gravenhurst. The onset of the Depression in 1929 saw a dwindling number of tourists coming to Muskoka each summer, and what was a flood just a few years before was reduced to a mere trickle. This coincided with the dawn of the automobile era, as well, which meant that the dependence travellers once had on steamships and trains was being eroded.

The loss of passenger and lumber business was driving trains, steamships, and the wharf to the edge of extinction. The Canadian National Railway gradually cut back its service to Muskoka, finally abandoning it entirely in 1952. One by one, the ships of the Muskoka Lakes Navigation Company were retired from service. The

Segwun and *Sagamo* docked at Muskoka Wharf, *circa* 1950s.
Courtesy of Muskoka Boat and Heritage Centre.

last steamship on the lakes, *Sagamo*, was retired from service in 1958. When the ship was permanently moored along the docks, the wharf grew eerily silent — obsolete and seemingly without a future. A year later, the once-bustling railway station at Muskoka Wharf was demolished.

It was inevitable that Gravenhurst should feel the loss, and not just on a sentimental level. The wharf had brought prosperity and lured thousands of tourists to the area, even in the waning years of the steamship era. When the ships were laid-up, numerous businesses dependent on tourism suffered economic downturn or closed outright. In time, Gravenhurst recovered, but it was never the same.

Until now, that is. In the last decade, an 89-acre development featuring boutique shops, restaurants, playgrounds, sporting fields, and lakeside boardwalks has restored a lustre to Muskoka Wharf not seen since the days when Gravenhurst was known as the Gateway to Muskoka. The Muskoka Boat and Heritage Centre, a state-of-the-art museum, offers the opportunity to explore the history of the steamships and luxury hotels that defined this region. The centre includes a number of interactive exhibits, including North America's largest collection of in-water antique wooden boats. Overlooking the entire wharf, and just 70 feet from the shore, is the newly built Residence Inn by Marriott. From here, all the attractions are just a few minutes away. And at the end of a day of exploring, one can retire to a private balcony, pull up a Muskoka chair, and gaze out onto the placid waters as *Segwun* or her sister ship, the newly built *Wenonah II*, slowly glide into view.

The steamships no longer dock at the old Muskoka Wharf. Today, that location is occupied by a line of unsightly boathouses that do little to remind us of the history that unfolded here. Instead, they dock a kilometre to the east, at the site of the original Gravenhurst town wharfs and the Muskoka Lakes Navigation Company's shipyards. But in a successful effort to conjure the magic of yesteryear, the ships' ticket office was built in the image of the lost Muskoka Wharf train station.

Muskoka Wharf today, with the Residence Inn and Muskoka Boat and Heritage Centre.
Courtesy of Residence Inn.

There is once again vibrancy at Muskoka Wharf. The development, still not complete, has transformed a moribund waterfront into perhaps the most exciting spot in Muskoka. In the past, Gravenhurst was the heart of the region. Its pulse slowed for a while with the demise of the lumber industry and the decline of the steamships, but now the beat is most definitely back.

Explore Muskoka Wharf

Sagamo Park

Sagamo Park was opened in 1986 in an attempt to beautify the historic waterfront and clean up the area. Visitors today find a beautiful expanse, with picnic tables and manicured gardens overlooking the water. In years past, things were much different.

For nearly a century, the Muskoka Lakes Navigation Company operated a shipyard on the site. It was a place of industry, not recreation. Never pretty in the best of times, as the company fortunes declined in the 20th century, the shipyard grew increasingly unsightly. The area was a tangled maze of rickety docks, weathered boathouses, storage sheds, heaps of worn-out machinery, rotting lumber, discarded ship parts, and other detritus.

Thankfully, Sagamo Park has succeeded in eliminating all evidence of this industrial wasteland, purging it so completely that few even realize the history that unfolded here. Every year, thousands of people happily mill about the park while awaiting their turn to board *Segwun* or *Sagamo*, perhaps admiring the beauty of the steamship's ticket office and interpretive centre that accurately recreate the original Muskoka Wharf Station.

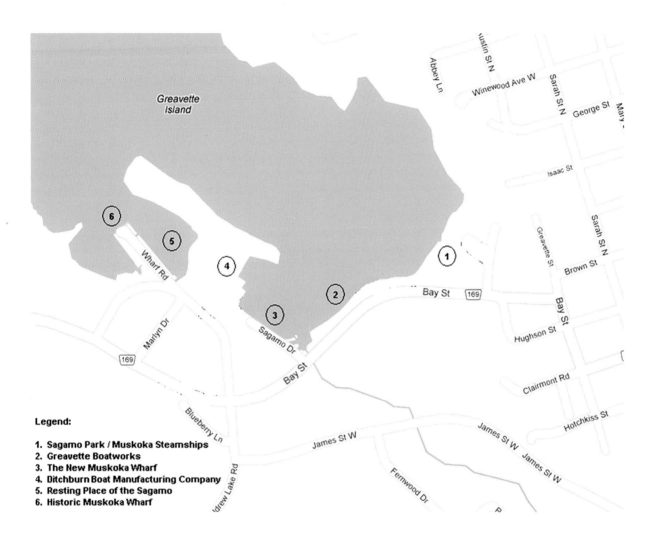

Legend:

1. Sagamo Park / Muskoka Steamships
2. Greavette Boatworks
3. The New Muskoka Wharf
4. Ditchburn Boat Manufacturing Company
5. Resting Place of the Sagamo
6. Historic Muskoka Wharf

Greavette Boatworks

The Greavette name was once almost synonymous with Muskoka boat building, and it was here, on a spot buried under modern-day Highway 169, that hundreds of sleek wooden motorboats were manufactured by Greavette Boats Ltd.

Company founder Tom Greavette learned his trade from Henry Ditchburn, a master craftsman regarded by many as the father of Muskoka boat building. Greavette began his own company in 1931 and was one of the first boat manufacturers in Muskoka to try assembly-line construction. He envisioned building a boat a day, but the Depression made such ambitious plans little more than a pipe dream. Instead, he turned to the custom-designed boats that made him famous. Two of Greavette's boats, *Little Miss Canada* and *Miss Canada*, built for Muskoka racing legend Harold Wilson, captured national and international attention during the 1930s.

During the Second World War, Greavette Boats built six 30- and 40-foot rescue boats for the Royal Canadian Air Force, which were transported by rail to larger waterways.

Tom Greavette died in 1958 and ownership passed first to his daughter Lorraine, then on to Bruce Wilson, who moved the plant to Port Carling in 1978, closing a chapter in the history of Muskoka Wharf. The former Greavette Boats building, leaning wearily and weathered by years of neglect, was torn down in 1987.

The New Muskoka Wharf

Today, the shoreline of Muskoka Bay is lined with boardwalks, restaurants, and shopping venues, part of the ambitious Muskoka Wharf development that has transformed a moribund stretch of lakefront into a vibrant tourist attraction. It's always alive with activity — couples strolling hand-in-hand, boats coming in to dock, diners engaged in lively conversations over drinks and good food, everyone enjoying the warm Muskoka sun and the pleasant views out over the water.

But go back 50 years or so, and we'll find activity of an entirely different sort here, the views far less appealing. During the heyday of lumbering (1870s to 1940s), the reek of smoke and rotting sawdust hung heavily in the air. The ear-splitting whine of more than a dozen saws echoed across the bay, and for as far as the eye could see were stockpiles of lumber and shingles and mounds of sawdust. Out on the bay was a wooden sargasso comprised of thousands of logs tangled together. The dozen or so sawmills that operated around the Muskoka Bay shoreline blocked the view of the surrounding hillsides with their rickety wooden superstructures and jack-ladder devices.

At various times, other industries were found here, as well, including the Gravenhurst Potash Works, with its towering concrete silos, and small boatworks that churned out wooden boats made by hand. All this conspired to make this among the more unsightly stretches of shoreline anywhere in Muskoka.

Thankfully, that is no longer the case, and the new Muskoka Wharf development is a worthy companion to the graceful *Segwun* docked nearby.

Ditchburn Boat Manufacturing Company

Henry Ditchburn was the undisputed father of boat building in Muskoka. He came from a long line of boat builders dating back to the 16th century, and gained considerable maritime experience as a member of the Royal Navy. Nevertheless, Ditchburn's entry into the boat-building industry began modestly enough. He and his brothers, William and Arthur, settled in Rosseau in 1869. W.H. Pratt, the owner of the Rosseau House Hotel, encouraged them to build rowboats and canoes for guests of his establishment. After the hotel burned down in 1883, Henry organized a boat-building and rental business, which he operated from a shop near the Rosseau wharf.

Around 1890, Ditchburn moved his company to Gravenhurst, where he built a large wooden boat factory just a stone's throw from Muskoka Wharf Station. This building was razed by fire in 1915, but was replaced with a new brick building, built on the same foundations.

After Henry's death, the company passed to his ambitious nephew Herbert, who established branch operations throughout Muskoka. Profits rolled in as the company crafted luxury yachts for millionaires, such as the *Kawandag* for Sir John Eaton in 1916. Before the Depression, Herbert Ditchburn began a major expansion project and invested heavily in it. He was crushed when the stock market crash ruined his plans and bankrupted the company. His attempts to start a new company met with limited success, and by 1938 the operation had closed for good.

Today, the site of the Ditchburn Boat Manufacturing Company is occupied by the Residence Inn. Opened in 2009, this welcoming hotel boasts 44 suites (almost all with balconies overlooking the water), an indoor pool and whirlpool, and other amenities designed to encourage people to linger in Muskoka Wharf.

Resting Place of Sagamo

Lying submerged in a watery grave between the Muskoka Wharf and a ridge of rock to the right are the rusted remains of the once palatial *Sagamo*. It's lain there so long that most people have forgotten it's there at all; certainly, there's no marker indicating the ship's location.

A bird's-eye view of Muskoka Wharf today. One of the region's most vibrant locations, it now boasts shops, restaurants, and the Muskoka Steamship and Heritage Museum in addition to numerous recreational opportunities and breathtaking scenery.
Courtesy of Residence Inn.

For more than 50 years, *Sagamo* served as the flagship of the Muskoka Lakes Navigation Company fleet, the largest and most lavishly outfitted vessel they had ever built. The ship had been out of service for a decade and was serving as a floating restaurant when it caught fire in 1969. The flames burned so hot they left nothing but the ship's metal ribbing behind. There was no thought of rebuilding her, and the remains of *Sagamo* were towed across Muskoka Bay to the very place where the steamer was launched to such fanfare in 1906.

Historic Muskoka Wharf

Today, a line of rather weary-looking boathouses occupies the point of land that was once the home of the famous Muskoka Wharf. While the tracks have long been lifted, it's not hard to imagine the trains slowly chugging right out onto this point and then hissing to a stop in a cloud of steam and smoke. Passengers would debark from their cars and walk just a few metres across to the steamers moored alongside. Mounds of luggage would follow, wheeled across the wharf on carts pushed by porters. It was a model of efficiency. The attractive ticket office, torn down in 1959, was located near the base of this point.

CHAPTER SIX

SHIPS OF THE MUSKOKA LAKES NAVIGATION COMPANY

From 1866 to 1958, the Muskoka Lakes Navigation Company operated 19 steamships on the Muskoka Lakes, making it the largest company of its kind on inland waters in Canada. Each of these vessels was unique in character, appearance, and history.

Ahmic

Built in 1896, the little steamer *Ahmic* (meaning "beaver") was originally a small tug intended to replace *Lake Joseph*, which had just been retired and sold by the company. For the first five years, *Ahmic* was used mostly for towing log booms and cargo scows, though she was also available for special charters. Often she would be tasked with towing the houseboat *Victoria*, which the company had outfitted to accommodate fishing parties.

As the towing business declined, the "Amy," as *Ahmic* was affectionately known by her crew, increasingly took on the role of passenger steamer. To better facilitate that role, over the winter of 1902–03 the vessel was

The *Ahmic*, pictured here at Port Carling, was a hard-working tug and supply vessel until she was remodelled to serve as a passenger steamer. Modest compared to the more famed steamers of the Muskoka Navigation Company, she nonetheless plied the lakes for half a century.
Courtesy of Muskoka Boat and Heritage Centre.

lengthened and a second deck was added. While this reconstruction dramatically increased her carrying capacity, it also made her notoriously top-heavy and unstable. Passengers also complained that the lack of a hurricane deck meant they had to crowd below on the freight deck when the weather was bad. A hurricane deck was finally added in 1904–05, but nothing could be done to remedy her tendency of rolling when heavily loaded.

Despite public fears regarding her safety, *Ahmic* operated incident-free for most of her 44 years. The closest she came to disaster was July 7, 1943, when she was holed after striking a submerged post at the mouth of the Muskoka River. She rapidly began to fill with water and had to be beached on Birch Island to avoid sinking.

Repaired, *Ahmic* sailed until 1949. She was broken up at Gravenhurst two years later.

Charlie M.

As business swelled around the turn of the century, the Muskoka Lakes Navigation Company found itself hard-pressed to keep up with demand in the busy summer months. In 1903, they decided to add another auxiliary steamer to the fleet to complement *Ahmic*. This vessel was the *Charlie M.*

Charlie M. had been built six years earlier as the personal yacht of Charles Mickle, co-owner of the Mickle and Dyment Lumber Company, one of the largest companies of its kind in Ontario and owners of a massive mill on the Gravenhurst waterfront.

The *Charlie M.* had a powerful engine that made her very fast for her time, capable of sustained steaming at an impressive 14 miles per hour. She was used primarily for special charters in the peak season of July and August, but never proved popular with passengers, who had to climb over the side rails to get aboard. During a 1907 reconstruction, this problem was fixed when she was lengthened to 74 feet.

Her demise was mysterious. Somehow during the night of July 6, 1919, she caught fire while docked at Gravenhurst. By the time anyone noticed the flames, it was too late; by morning she had become a sunken, useless hulk. The *Charlie M.* rests under landfill at the Gravenhurst waterfront.

Cherokee

Cherokee was essentially a smaller version of *Sagamo*, and as such was touted as a "palace steamer." Graceful, boasting elegant lounges and the latest amenities, she was a favourite with the public and was the most requested boat when charters were booked.

The ship had a steel hull, which had been built in Toronto but assembled in Gravenhurst in the spring and early summer of 1907. She was launched on July 17, though she did not enter service until the following year. Though significantly smaller than *Sagamo*, *Cherokee* could easily accommodate 400 passengers. She proved to have a near flawless design, save for one weakness: her boilers and engines were set forward, making her heavy in the bow and light in the stern, which caused her to plow through the water.

Starting in 1931 she became known as the "Sunset Cruiser," taking passengers from lakeside hotels to Port Carling for evening dances. Such cruises were extremely popular during the height of the Big Band Era, but one of these nighttime cruises almost ended in disaster in mid-August 1932.

It was already dark and rainy when *Cherokee* picked up passengers at the Royal Muskoka, Wigwassan, and Windermere resorts. On the return trip the rain was coming down in sheets and visibility was near zero. Driving winds pushed the ship off course and she ran aground on a shoal near Monyca Island. The hull plates gave and the forward compartment flooded, and there was very real concern that the ship might sink. Thankfully, before dawn, *Cherokee* slipped loose and the crew managed to control the flooding long enough to allow the ship to limp back to Rosseau.

Passengers board the *Cherokee* at Port Carling, perhaps for the 100-Mile Cruise, *circa* 1950s. The *Ahmic* is docked behind.
Courtesy of Muskoka Boat and Heritage Centre.

Cherokee survived this brush with disaster and went on to serve on the lakes until she was retired in 1950. In 1961 she succumbed to the wrecker's ball; however, her wheelhouse and officer's cabins were spared and are now on display at the Muskoka Boat and Heritage Centre.

Islander

The *Islander* bears the distinction of being the last vessel built for the company to be a wood-burner. More impressive is her record of 51 straight seasons plying the Muskoka lakes, a number unequalled by any other steamship.

Built in 1900, *Islander* was a composite steamer, with a steel frame and a wooden hull. The frame and machinery had been built in Toronto but were assembled in Muskoka, where the hull was added. For her size she drew a lot of water (5.7 feet), which made her very steady and easy to steer on a straight course — this was especially important at night or in foggy or rainy weather. Indeed, she was so steady on the compass that the captain could sometimes tie the wheel in place and let her steer herself! On the other hand, *Islander* proved cumbersome and heavy to turn.

Unlike most of the ships in the fleet, *Islander* was never enlarged and only was only occasionally remodelled. In 1904, for example, a lounge cabin was installed on her upper deck. By the 1920s, her machinery was replaced so that she could burn coal.

The *Islander* proved extremely efficient and popular with the public, and sailed for five uninterrupted decades. Her sailing days came to an end in 1950 when an inspection revealed dry rot in her timbers and she was deemed unfit to carry passengers. Four years later she was sold and turned into a barge, but was broken up in 1958. Her wheelhouse is now preserved at the Muskoka Boat and Heritage Centre.

The *Islander* majestically sails toward the dock at Beaumaris Resort in 1945.
Courtesy of Muskoka Boat and Heritage Centre.

Kenozha

In her day, *Kenozha* (meaning "pickerel") enjoyed the title of fastest ship in the Muskoka Lakes Navigation Company fleet. She was also said to be the company's most efficient and economical vessel, able to sail 100 miles and carry 250 passengers on just two cords of wood. And with her smooth handling and handsome appearance, she was a favourite with the public. In short, *Kenozha* was arguably the most successful vessel ever built for the company.

Launched in 1883 to replace the burned *Wenonah*, a year later she enjoyed the honour of conducting A.P. Cockburn and the governor general, the Marquis of Lansdowne, on a tour of the Muskoka Lakes. The ever-increasing demand for space aboard Muskoka's steamships compelled the Muskoka Lakes Navigation Company to dramatically remodel *Kenozha* in 1898, with her hull being lengthening by nearly 20 feet, making her, until the arrival of the *Medora* in 1903, the largest ship in the fleet.

The *Kenozha* didn't lead an entirely charmed existence, however. On August 11, 1908, she collided with the massive *Sagamo* at Beaumaris and suffered a crushed forepeak. Both the skipper and his mate were fired for the embarrassing and costly accident.

Worse was to follow a decade later. On August 15, 1918, *Kenozha* was docked for the night at Stanley House on northern Lake Joseph. The crew was sound asleep in their bunks when someone smelled smoke and sounded the alarm. The crew of 14 barely had time to abandon ship before the inferno engulfed the vessel, and the captain was forced to dive overboard in his nightshirt with crackling flames nipping at his heels.

Once the crew was safely ashore, the ship was cut loose from the dock; it floated off, grounding on the north side of Stanley Bay, where it burned to the waterline and sank.

The *Kenozha*, in 1909, a year after she collided with *Sagamo*. Her forecastle was crushed in the accident, but after being rebuilt, the ship had a long career on the lakes.
Courtesy of Muskoka Boat and Heritage Centre.

Lake Joseph

The title of most unusual-looking vessel in the company fleet belongs, hands-down, to the tug *Lake Joseph*. She was built with an experimental V-shaped bottom that designers hoped would allow her to cut more easily through water, making her faster. It didn't work. More immediately noticeable was the fact that the vessel lacked a wheelhouse.

Entering the fleet in 1881, *Lake Joseph* spent 15 years towing logs across the lakes. She has the distinction of being the last of the Muskoka Lakes Navigation Company tugs. Sold in 1896 to Andrew Boyd, a prominent lumberman who owned a sawmill at Cedar Beach, near Milford Bay, the ship spent a few more seasons running under his name.

The *Lake Joseph*'s end came in memorable fashion one night in 1899. A fire started suddenly in the boiler room, and before anyone could react, flames had jumped to the pile of fuel wood. Dense smoke and intense heat hindered efforts to fight the fire, leaving the captain with no choice but to run the ship aground and abandon her to her fate.

Medora

The *Medora*, built in 1893 in response to a growing tourist trade, was named in honour of Medora Playfair, the wife of John S. Playfair, then vice-president of the Muskoka Lakes Navigation Company. The *Medora* was designed for size and opulence; at 122 feet in length and 25 feet in beam, she was as large as the original lock system at Port Carling could handle. She was also the first composite steamer in the fleet, with a wooden hull built around a steel frame.

The company had high hopes for their newest vessel, but she had an inauspicious start to her career when, during her maiden voyage on June 28, 1893, her propeller snapped on a piece of floating timber shortly after she left the wharf. The ship had to be towed back to the dock — still lined with VIPs and company shareholders.

Thankfully, things turned around and she eventually became the pride of the fleet, a ship known for her comfort and seaworthiness. It was fitting, therefore, that when the governor general of Canada, Lord Aberdeen, and his wife decided to toured the lakes in 1898 they would do so aboard the *Medora*.

In 1901–02, the *Medora* was enlarged and lengthened by 20 feet, making her the largest ship on the lakes until *Sagamo* appeared in 1906. After the amendments, she could accommodate 359 passengers and enough freight to fill five railway cars. On the flipside of the coin, the ship was very heavy, making her difficult to steer. This was compounded by the fact that she was still equipped with hand gears rather than steam-powered steering. In light of her size and sluggish handling, the crew began to affectionately call her "The Moose."

After the onset of the Great Depression, the *Medora* was retired in 1931 and placed in dry dock. Over the following decade she began to deteriorate, and was gutted by a fire set by young boys on June 1, 1940. After that, there was no hope that the ship would ever sail again, and in 1947 the hulk was sold for scrap.

Mink (see Waome)

Muskoka

The steamship *Muskoka* began her existence as a tug, replacing the retired *Simcoe*. She was far better suited to the role than her predecessor. Though very slow (her maximum speed being eight miles per hour), the *Muskoka* was more than twice the size of *Simcoe* and far more powerful, allowing her to tow bigger log booms and thereby reap greater profits for the company. Her immense strength also meant she was the first steamer to break through the ice in the springtime, and the *Muskoka*'s appearance on the lakes heralded the coming of a new season for settlers and was greatly anticipated each year.

Although built as a tug, she gradually evolved into a passenger steamer over the course of several rounds of reconstruction throughout the 1890s. Altogether, she went through a least five different upgrades. The most extensive reconstruction occurred in 1897–98, when she was lengthened from 94 to 110 feet and given a new boiler that improved her speed to 12 miles per hour. The *Muskoka* was all but unrecognizable as the tug she had once been, and while still unattractive, her capacity of 200 passengers made her a welcome addition to a fleet struggling to keep up with demand.

By 1907, the aging vessel leaking and her machinery worn, she was pulled from service. The *Muskoka* was kept on-hand for a few more years as an emergency fill-in for other steamers, but was officially retired from service in 1912.

The steamship *Muskoka*, docked at Muskoka Wharf. Her 26-year career ended in 1907, after her aging timbers had made her increasingly unseaworthy. Her replacement in the fleet was the legendary *Sagamo*.
Courtesy of Muskoka Boat and Heritage Centre.

Nipissing

The first flagship of the Muskoka Lakes Navigation Company fleet was *Nipissing* (meaning "little body of water"), a sidewheeler built at Gravenhurst in 1871. Her design was copied from the *Emily May*, at the time the most attractive steamer on Lake Simcoe.

A few short years after her launch, the ship had the honour of conducting the governor general, the Earl Dufferin, and his countess on their 1874 tour of the Muskoka Lakes. The *Nipissing* was refitted in 1877, with a third hurricane deck and a second lounge cabin being added.

On August 3, 1886, *Nipissing* was docked for the night at Port Cockburn, on the northern end of Lake Joseph. Around 4:00 a.m., a fire broke out near the boiler room and swiftly engulfed the ship. Crew members, chased from their bunks, barely had time to abandon ship; some, finding the gangways already a mass of flames, were forced to climb out the nearest window and jumped overboard in their nightshirts.

Fearing that the flames might jump from the ship to the wharf-side freight sheds and perhaps even the nearby Summit House hotel, the crew hastily cast off the lines and pushed the burning ship away from the docks. They watched as *Nipissing* grounded near Fraser Island and burned to the waterline. It was said that the blaze was so intense that it cast a red glow on the horizon that could be seen from as far away as the south end of Lake Joseph.

The *Nipissing*'s engines and boiler were salvaged and installed in a second *Nipissing*, the current *Segwun*. The remainder of her hull was sunk and is still visited by divers today.

Oriole

The *Oriole* was added to the company fleet in 1886 to replace *Wenonah*, which had burned in spectacular fashion. An attractive little ship, she was famous for her octagonal, pagoda-style wheelhouse topped by a beautifully carved wooden oriole. Her small size made her ideal for assuming the Muskoka River route into Bracebridge, but the *Oriole* was not a popular ship because her narrow beam gave her a tendency to roll heavily and passengers feared she would capsize.

The evening of June 30, 1889, saw Lake Muskoka draped in a heavy curtain of fog as the *Oriole* slowly sailed into Muskoka Bay. At 12:30 a.m., the ship sliced through a small boat full of people that had suddenly crossed in front of its bow. Bodies flew into the water. The *Oriole*'s crew managed to rescue five people, but two women and one little girl were swallowed up by fog and water and drowned.

Fears regarding the *Oriole*'s stability proved well-founded. On May 2, 1904, the heavily overloaded ship rolled over while rounding the Devil's Elbow, a bend in the Muskoka River about half a mile below the wharf in Bracebridge. The ship sank to the riverbed, but thankfully this time no lives were lost, and passengers and crew were able to escape before she slipped beneath the water.

The *Oriole* was raised and continued to run until 1927, when she was replaced by the *Mink*. She was broken up for scrap a year later.

Rosseau

When *Waubamik* was retired in 1879, the company began searching for another small steamer that could be used to tow logs to area sawmills. They found a yacht already under construction at Gravenhurst, purchased her, and named her *Rosseau*.

The *Rosseau* was used as a tug and scow boat, but on occasion took passengers for pleasure cruises or private charters. Her skipper, the son of a prominent mill owner, was Captain George Bailey, a young man who went on to become one of the most respected and longest-serving officers in the Muskoka Lakes Navigation Company.

The *Rosseau* wasn't a member of the fleet for long, and in 1882 she was sold to the Muskoka Leather Company of Bracebridge, which used her to tow scows loaded with tanbark, a material essential for curing leather hides. She was sold again in 1899, this time to the Snider Lumber Company, which operated a mill at Rosseau Falls. She plied the Muskoka Lakes until 1915, when she was subsequently scuttled.

Sagamo

The *Sagamo* (meaning "big chief") was a palace steamer and the pride of the Muskoka Lakes for half a century. In her day, she was the largest passenger ship on any inland waterway in Ontario with the exception of the Ottawa River.

Sagamo was a floating palace, easily the largest and most extravagant steamship to sail the inland waterways of Ontario. Nearly twice the size of *Segwun*, she could comfortably carry up to 400 passengers.
Courtesy of Muskoka Boat and Heritage Centre.

Entering service in 1907, and built in response to the phenomenal growth of the resort industry, she boasted four decks, four lifeboats, three spacious lounges, electric lighting, and a dining room capable of seating 90 patrons. In total, she could accommodate 800 passengers. The *Sagamo* was as big as any other two ships on the Muskoka Lakes combined and required a crew of 26; yet she was also the fastest, capable of reaching speeds of 18 miles per hour.

On September 9, 1925, a fire broke out aboard the ship during the layup at season's end in Gravenhurst. Except for the dining room, most of the vessel's wooden superstructure was destroyed before the blaze could be brought under control. It was a devastating blow to the company. Nevertheless, the majestic ship was rebuilt in time for the 1926 season. During the reconstruction the ship was fitted out with 15 staterooms for guests who wished to spend the night aboard, the first on the Muskoka Lakes to have such accommodations.

By the late 1950s, *Sagamo* was the last steamship operating in Muskoka. But even this mighty vessel couldn't resist the tides of history, and on Labour Day 1958, she sailed for the final time.

In the years following, efforts were made to convert her into a floating restaurant. In fact, on January 10, 1969, she was in the process of being painted when a fire broke out onboard. For the second time in her history she was gutted by flames, but this time there would be no restoration. The *Sagamo* was deemed beyond salvage and the remains of her hull were buried under landfill at the site of the old Muskoka Wharf.

Simcoe

Originally called the *M.C. Simons*, this sturdy little tug was built at Buffalo, New York, in 1866. She was reputed to have been used as a gunboat, patrolling the Niagara River during the Fenian Raids of the time, but what's certain is that in 1868 she was taken to Lake Simcoe to tow logs to the sawmill at Belle Ewart, located on the lake's western shore.

The tug served in this capacity until purchased by the Muskoka Lakes Navigation Company in 1875 and shipped by railcar to Gravenhurst. Renamed *Simcoe*, she replaced *Waubamik* and was used mainly for towing logs to the Gravenhurst sawmills, though she also handled passengers and cargo on occasion.

The *Simcoe* was noted for her speed, and during an 1876 regatta on Lake Rosseau she handily beat the much larger *Nipissing* in a race to the Indian River that thrilled hundreds of spectators. Four years later, however, *Simcoe* was deemed unseaworthy and was broken up at Gravenhurst, replaced by the new tugs *Muskoka* and *Lake Joseph*.

Waome

The last addition to the Muskoka Lakes Navigation Company fleet was *Waome* (meaning "water lily"), a small auxiliary steamer. The vessel was launched as the *Mink* in 1912 by the William Hanna Company of Port Carling, who employed her as a supply boat and floating store. By 1925, the William Hanna Company was operating only its larger supply ship, *Newminko*, leaving the *Mink* tied up for several seasons at Port Carling.

The Muskoka Lakes Navigation Company purchased her in 1927 to replace the aging *Oriole*, gave her a new name, and remodelled her, adding a lounge cabin on the upper deck. Like *Oriole* and *Ahmic*, *Waome* was used mostly on side-runs, such as on Lake Joseph or the Muskoka River.

Long overshadowed by her larger sister ships, *Waome* grabbed the headlines for herself on October 6, 1934. The day was cold, dark, and overcast, the heavy clouds on the horizon promising rain. Around 10:00 a.m., *Waome* pulled away from the dock at Port Carling bound for Beaumaris at the northern end of Lake Muskoka. Aboard were six crewmen and a single passenger. A light rain was falling, but there was no reason to believe there was any danger in setting sail. What no one could know was that a freak storm with hurricane-force winds was blowing down trees near Bala — and heading in their direction.

Half an hour later, while on open water, a tremendous gust of wind caught the little steamer broadside and instantly rolled her onto her side. In less than a minute she had been swallowed up by the lake, dragging the lone passenger and a crewman with her. Those crew members who made it off the ship found themselves in a desperate fight for survival. The water was bitterly cold, waves were four feet high, and there was no one around to help them — most cottagers had already left for the season. The desperate swim for shore claimed a third victim.

The *Waome* sits upright in 80 feet of water, a rusting tombstone for the three victims and a reminder of the worst maritime disaster in Muskoka's history.

Waubamik

The second steamer to appear in Muskoka, *Waubamik* (meaning "white beaver") was a propeller-driven vessel built in Buffalo in 1866 and originally known as the *Dean*. The following year she was brought to Lakes Couchiching and Simcoe, where she carried passengers and freight and towed logs for a number of seasons.

In 1869, A.P. Cockburn purchased the steamship to supplement *Wenonah*. With the railway not yet extending to Gravenhurst, there was little choice but to painstakingly drag the vessel over the Muskoka Road. That winter, *Waubamik* was loaded onto a custom-made sleigh and hauled north by two teams of horses. Often, crews would have to stop to cut the trees along the road to create enough clearance for the ship to pass. Progress was agonizingly slow, but by spring *Waubamik* was moored alongside *Wenonah* and ready for the sailing season.

Muskoka Lakes Navigation Company

The Muskoka Lakes Navigation Company has gone by various corporate names over the past century and a half of its existence. A brief timeline is as follows:

1866 – A.P. Cockburn launches the steamer *Wenonah*. As far as is known, this early operation was not incorporated.

1881 – Cockburn's company, which has several steamers on Lake Nipissing in addition to those on the Muskoka Lakes, is incorporated as the Muskoka and Nipissing Navigation Company.

1889 – By this time, the company has given up its Lake Nipissing branch but was running steamers on Georgian Bay. It is renamed the Muskoka and Georgian Bay Navigation Company.

1903 – Following the withdrawal of the Georgian Bay service, the company builds the Royal Muskoka Hotel on Lake Rosseau. It then becomes the Muskoka Lakes Navigation and Hotel Company Limited.

1958 – The company dissolves with the retirement of the last operating steamers and the destruction by fire of the Royal Muskoka Hotel.

1981 – The name and charter of the Muskoka Lakes Navigation and Hotel Company Limited is revived by the Muskoka Steamship and Historical Society to operate the restored RMS *Segwun*.

Later that year, she was portaged past the rapids at Port Carling (the locks there were still under construction at the time), giving her the distinction of being the first steamer on Lake Rosseau. The *Waubamik* served on this lake until she was sold in 1876.

The new owner, Captain Joseph Huckins, had her hauled overland once again, this time to Baysville. She was renamed *Dean* and became the first steamship to sail on Lake of Bays. She was active there for four or five years, but her ultimate fate is unknown. It's believed she was scuttled around 1881 and lies somewhere within the shadowy depths of the lake.

Wenonah

The first steamship to appear in Muskoka, A.P. Cockburn appropriately gave this sidewheeler a name that means "first born" in the Ojibwa language. The *Wenonah* was built at Gravenhurst in 1866, and originally featured decks that were open to the elements. Following complaints from passengers, a hurricane deck was added in time for the 1867 sailing season.

The *Wenonah* ferried freight and passengers around the lakes and towed logs to area sawmills, generally with A.P. Cockburn himself at the helm. She suffered more accidents and groundings than any ship in the company's fleet because the waterways were then largely uncharted; navigational hazards were discovered the hard way.

After 20 years of service, her wooden hull was worn, and after a short stint as a houseboat she was abandoned at Cinderwood Island, near Beaumaris. She was later scuttled nearby, though not before her engines were removed and installed in a new *Wenonah*, built at Burk's Falls in 1886 to serve on the Magnetawan River in the central Parry Sound District.

CHAPTER SEVEN

OFFICERS AND CREW

While the captain and engineer were the most well-known and prestigious individuals aboard any steamship, there were as many as a dozen other officer and crew positions that had to be filled to ensure that the ship ran efficiently and that the passengers had an enjoyable experience.

Captain

The captain was in charge of all aspects of the ship under his command, most notably piloting and navigating. The many shoals and rocks on the Muskoka Lakes meant it was especially important for captains to have good local knowledge.

Cook

The cook was responsible for planning meals; ordering supplies; preparing breakfast, lunch, high tea, and dinner for both passengers and crew; and for directing the kitchen staff.

Deckhand

The deckhand's primary responsibility was to assist with docking, which may have included throwing the lines for tethering. The deckhand was also responsible for keeping the ship clean and neat. Before the days of electricity, the deckhand would ensure the ship had a full supply of ice and would obtain a supply from the ice house at the wharf. The deckhand would also be required to take the mailbags by rowboat to the resorts and other locations along the route as needed.

Engineer

The engineer ensured that the engines, boiler, and all mechanical components of the ship were in good working order and properly maintained. He would operate the engines according to the instructions of the captain through telegraph communication — forward, reverse, fast, slow.

Fireman

The fireman's job was to stoke the boilers with fuel, which could be either wood or coal. Many firemen also served as oilers (see below).

Mate

The mate was responsible for assuming command of the vessel when the captain was dining or otherwise unavailable. The mate would also be responsible for the overall direction of the crew; ensuring the neatness and cleanliness of the ship; and supervising docking from the main deck, including setting the gangplanks according to captain's instructions. In addition, the mate would ensure that all freight, baggage, mail, and supplies were onboard or removed at the correct docking places, and was responsible for the completion of minor repairs.

Newsstand Boy

The "newsie" was considered an officer on the ship and would operate a confection stand where newspapers and light refreshments were sold.

Oiler

The oiler was responsible for the continuous oiling of all engines and mechanical moving parts as well as filling the oil and grease cups under the direction of the engineer.

Purser

The purser's duties consisted of greeting and assisting the passengers, collecting their tickets, as well as making dining arrangements. The purser also had to manage the freight and the main deck and oversee the steamships' Royal Mail Service. Last but not least, they also had to oversee the activities of the dining room and staterooms.

Red Caps

Red caps would handle the luggage for passengers as they boarded or disembarked the train and ship. Since many passengers would spend their entire summer in Muskoka, each could have as many as 15 to 20 trunks for the red caps to handle. All of their income came from tips.

Stewardess

The deck stewardess was responsible for the comfort and needs of passengers while on deck, including providing them with water and blankets. The stateroom stewardess was responsible for making up the stateroom and ensuring it was clean and tidy.

Stores keeper

The stores keeper worked primarily on the wharf and would maintain stores of food supplies needed on the ships. The stores keeper would receive a list of requirements from the cook, go back to stores to fill the order, load the supplies on a cart, and then take it down to the wharf to the ship. The stores keeper would also reorder supplies from wholesalers.

Waitress

Waitresses were required to wear white uniforms and caps as well as hair nets. Each waitress would be responsible for up to six tables in the dining room, serving passengers and crew breakfast, lunch, afternoon tea, and dinner. Additional duties included setting tables, polishing silver and glassware, and miscellaneous kitchen jobs if needed.

CHAPTER EIGHT

THE RMS *SEGWUN*

et's jump forward a bit. It's the middle of the Roaring Twenties, the First World War is over, and prosperity has returned, stretching out across the horizon to create an unharnessed sense of optimism. In Muskoka, the summer resorts are doing a booming business and the steamships of the Muskoka Lakes Navigation Company fleet are once again sailing to full capacity, their holds full of cargo and their rails lined with thrilled passengers. It seems that even with the growing number of private motorboats on the lakes, and automobiles offering an alternate source of transportation, there is no slowing down the steamships. Business is good. In fact, it's great.

With so much activity in the waterways, it seemed that even with six steamers in commission the company was not fully serving its clients, nor reaching its full potential. Managers thought a seventh steamship was needed; but why build a new one when they had *Nipissing II* waiting in the wings, long unused but still seaworthy? So during the fall and winter of 1924, repair crews went to work on the old ship, preparing her to join the fleet the following season.

Over the winter, the boiler and engines were removed, as were the sidewalls, pontoons, and paddlewheels. The *Nipissing*'s aged machinery was useless — it was the reason she had been pulled from service a decade earlier — but the old iron hull and portions of the superstructure were still in fine shape. A new marine boiler from St. Catharines was put into place, along with two reciprocating double-expansion compound engines, both made in Goderich, Ontario. The old ship, meanwhile, was converted to twin propellers.

Much of the interior remained untouched, however, including the woodwork, the forward lounge, the steering wheel, and the whistle. What emerged that spring was a handsome new sightseeing steamer that

Segwun pulls up to the wharf at Elgin House circa late 1940s. Even after many of Muskoka's resorts were forced to close after the Second World War, the Elgin House flourished, and *Segwun* continued to call.
Courtesy of Muskoka Boat and Heritage Centre.

complimented the other ships of the fleet but bore little resemblance to the old *Nipissing II*. Because she looked like a new vessel, the company decided to give her a new name as well. They chose to call her *Segwun*, an Ojibwa word meaning "springtime." And how appropriate, since not only was she was ready to sail in the spring of 1925, but the re-launch represented a new season in the old ship's history.

On July 9, 1925, *Segwun* set off on her maiden voyage to Bracebridge under the command of Captain A.P. Larson of Gravenhurst.[1] Her arrival was greeted with much excitement and applause. It must have been quite the site to see this beautiful new steamship slowly gliding across the water of the Muskoka River, flags flying high. She was docked majestically along the wharf, where excited passengers waited patiently to board. Bracebridge would be *Segwun*'s home port for many years.

It wasn't long before *Segwun* became a regular sight from the shore as she began her new route down the Muskoka River from Bracebridge to Beaumaris, where she would meet her sister ships, *Sagamo* from Gravenhurst and *Islander* from Bala. Sometimes *Cherokee* would also be on hand to exchange passengers, mail, and cargo. *Segwun* continued to call at Milford Bay and Port Keewaydin before steaming into Bala Bay to connect with the noon train. After that, she would return to Beaumaris, where she would once again meet up with *Sagamo* and *Islander*. Finally, deserving a rest after a long day sailing the lakes, *Segwun*'s crew would return to Bracebridge for the night. However, on nights when there were particularly large groups of people, *Segwun* would be called into service to escort *Sagamo* from the Muskoka Wharf, and for many years either *Segwun* or *Cherokee* would host a popular sunset cruise on the lake.

Segwun was typically the first ship launched each year and the last to be put to rest in the autumn. In early May the ship would enter service, taking the main route up the lake until the larger steamers were launched, taking up the slack and allowing her a more reduced load. These larger ships would generally stop running around Labour Day, but *Segwun* would continue to operate into October, once more taking over the main routes.

It's no wonder the RMS *Segwun* was such a popular ship. In addition to being attractive, she was also fast and smooth, having been designed with the engines set far enough back so that at high speed she planed above the water rather than ploughing through it like some of the other steamships. This made *Segwun* undeniably the fastest ship in her fleet, and she could easily cruise at 20 miles an hour. In fact, it was widely suspected that since *Segwun* was such a fast vessel, the company had her dry docked and fitted with new propellers to slow her down. They didn't like the idea that when *Segwun* raced against *Sagamo*, the fleet's flagship and pride and joy was left behind like old news.

Segwun's good fortune, and that of the Muskoka Lakes Navigation Company as a whole, was struck a serious blow on October 29, 1929, a date known ever since as "Black Tuesday." When the bottom fell out of the New York Stock Exchange and ushered in the dark decade of the Depression, it didn't take long for the shockwave to reach Muskoka. Small businesses closed, prices sagged, people were thrown out of work, and spirits plummeted. The luxury of a summer vacation was now beyond the reach of most people, and the annual influx of tourists dried up like crops in a withering drought. This, naturally, was a devastating turn of events for Muskoka's resorts, and many were forced to close. Needless to say, as tourism waned, it meant fewer passengers for *Segwun* and her sisters. The company muddled on, but the 1930s were far from a golden era for the company.

Things began to rebound toward the end of the decade, however, and even the outbreak of the Second World War in 1939 did little to slow its revival. Indeed, while the nation may have been involved in a global conflict, tourism picked up appreciably. By the end of the war, Canada had more than rebounded from the Depression of six years earlier. Real earnings had more than doubled, so people had more money to spend and, buoyed by the excitement of the end of the war, were very eager to spend it. Bright days were ahead, company officials reasoned, and so it was time to reinvest in the fleet.

In 1945–46, *Segwun* was pulled onto dry land in Gravenhurst for a much-needed overhaul, due largely to the rising demand for staterooms to accommodate guests. So with this in mind, the company decided to remove both

Segwun, pictured here in 1947. Note the open door, through which both passengers and cargo entered.
Courtesy of Muskoka Boat and Heritage Centre.

the ladies' lounge and the gentlemen's lounge on the promenade deck and use the space to install a large cabin section. Seven staterooms, each with toilets and double beds, were included in the new accommodations. During the renovations, the two original stairwells were also removed and a new one installed just in front of the boiler room. By 1951, hydrants and hoses had also been installed aboard *Segwun*, a reaction to the horrific fire that struck the SS *Noronic* in Toronto Harbour in 1949 that claimed more than a hundred lives.[2]

All this costly work was undertaken with the expectation that the glory days of the company were about to return. Unfortunately, they didn't. In the past, good times nationally had meant good times for the inland excursion steamships, but not this time. People no longer wanted to spend their leisure hours on a quiet, sedate passenger ship. Instead, they craved excitement and speed. To this new generation, steamboats seemed dull, old-fashioned, and out of step with the new mentality. People wanted to take vacations in exotic locations such as Europe, Florida, or the Caribbean. Muskoka was seen by many younger people as yesterday's news, a place more in tune with the pace of their parents' or grandparents' lifestyles than their own.

So tourism in the region dropped, and many hotels were forced to close. Compounding these problems was the network of paved highways invading Muskoka. All the road upgrading, extending the already paved networks of southern Ontario, reflected the growing preeminence of the automobile and undermined the role of the steamship.

As a result of these converging trends, all of Ontario's steamship lines began to wither away, disappearing one at a time over the course of the next decade or so. They were an anachronism, no longer vital or even seemingly wanted. None were destined to outlast the 1950s, the Muskoka Lakes Navigation Company included.

By the dawn of that decade, *Segwun* and *Sagamo* were the only steamships still sailing on the Muskoka Lakes. In 1951, *Segwun* stopped calling Bracebridge her home port and took on the route of its retired sister ship, *Cherokee*, plying the waters from Rosseau to Gravenhurst, meeting *Sagamo* at Port Carling twice a day. In 1955, the boats were purchased by Gravenhurst Steamships, and continued to sail for four more seasons under that name. Toward the end, *Segwun* sailed alone and began docking at Bala overnight — but all too often she sailed with empty decks.

But all good things must come to an end. The old steamer had given the district of Muskoka excellent service for more than 30 seasons since its re-launch and had, amazingly, avoided any serious accidents up until that time. In many ways she was a blessed ship, at least until 1958, when the veteran captain Ariss retired and a new captain was put in charge.[3] Suddenly, everything seemed to go wrong.

Segwun, docked at Beaumaris in the 1950s. The moody skies mirror the fortunes of the company during a time when it struggled to turn a profit due to lack of passengers.
Courtesy of Muskoka Boat and Heritage Centre.

The first trip of the season with new skipper saw *Segwun* driven against one of the wharves and into the lockmasters house above the Port Carling lock. The ship then rebounded off the wharf and struck the concrete section, bending her forepeak out of shape. Adding insult to injury, that same day she also bumped into the swing-bridge at Port Carling, almost knocking it off its base. It seemed that *Segwun* now had a spell of bad luck cast over her.

Mishap after mishap occurred with the new captain in charge. Somehow he managed to drive her into *Sagamo* and then damaged a motorboat docked at Beaumoris. Finally, on August 5, a junior wheelsman, ignoring instructions to take the ship through the middle of the channel between Point Montcalm and Browning Island on Lake Muskoka, managed to run the ship aground on Gull Rocks Shoal; before the engines could be shut down, two blades from one propeller and three on the other had been sheared off. Passengers were thrown about and many understandably panicked. Despite the impact, the ship was never in any danger of sinking; the old iron hull withstood the impact but the *Segwun* had to turn around and return to Gravenhurst at dead-slow speed. That trip proved to be her last, and her sister ship, *Sagamo*, finished the season. But after the Labour Day weekend, she, too, had sailed her last.

No one could have predicted that *Segwun* would be revived again. The end of the 1958 sailing season marked the end of the steamship era on the Muskoka Lakes. A 92-year tradition in the Muskoka District had come to an end, or so it seemed. And not just there; at the time, *Segwun* and *Sagamo* were among the last passenger steamships still running anywhere in Canada.

It was a sad development, and when *Segwun* was moored permanently along the docks, abandoned and lifeless, it looked as though the soul had been sucked from her. Was this really the end? While some things may not last forever, *Segwun* had not reached the end of her story quite yet. Those who continue to travel aboard her today know that there were still a few chapters left to be written.

CHAPTER NINE

THE 100-MILE CRUISE

At the dawn of the 1920s, the demand for steamships in Muskoka was in slow decline, largely owing to the fact that, with the improvement of roads and the onset of the automobile era, steamships no longer enjoyed a monopoly on transportation in the region. For the first time there was another way to move people and goods around the area. This development posed a long-term challenge to the Muskoka Lakes Navigation Company, one that might one day threaten its existence. It was vital that the company evolve and find new ways to ensure that steamships remained relevant in Muskoka well into the future.

Commodore Ralph W. Lee, skipper of *Sagamo*, believed he had a solution, and proposed a 100-mile excursion cruise that would encompass all three lakes.[1] The idea was that people would be encouraged to come to Muskoka not just to stay at the hotels but also to spend an entire day aboard ship. In short, boat trips would become an attraction in themselves rather than just a means of transportation to the hotels.

Lee expanded upon his vision when he suggested that the company purchase a property where passengers taking the all-day cruise could go ashore to stretch their legs and enjoy the untouched wilderness for an hour. More to the point, he believed he had the perfect location in mind — a stretch of undeveloped land at the head of a branch of Lake Joseph called Little Lake Joseph, which rose to a 100-foot rocky bluff overlooking the sparkling surface of Slide Lake (so called because lumbermen had once built a timber slide from this lake to Little Lake Joe).

Seeing the potential in Lee's plan, owners of the company purchased the wilderness property in 1923 and laid out a network of

A brochure featuring Muskoka Lakes Cruises. By the 1920s, the steamships of the Muskoka Navigation Company were increasingly turning to sightseeing cruises to remain relevant.
Courtesy of Muskoka Boat and Heritage Centre.

paths that transformed the location's tranquil setting. The property became known as Natural Park, and Slide Lake was given the more romantic and advertising-friendly name of Mirror Lake. That same year, the 100-Mile Cruise was born (though interestingly the route covered only 86 miles). It quickly became a success, and the 100-Mile Cruise became famous across North America as one of Ontario's foremost summer attractions. Its appeal was only enhanced when, starting sometime around 1931, Toronto pianist and big-band leader Charles Musgrave began providing musical entertainment and a lively commentary aboard *Sagamo* during the cruises.[2] He became as much a part of the experience as the blowing of the ship's whistle, and made sure to return to the ship every summer until his death in 1953.

The cruise became a beloved tradition. Passengers would travel by train from Toronto, spend the night aboard *Sagamo* (in spring and autumn, when numbers were lower, *Segwun* would often take her place), and be ready for the 7:00 a.m. departure time. Along the route, other ships, including *Segwun*, *Cherokee*, and *Medora*, would rendezvous with *Sagamo*, bringing additional passengers from Bracebridge, Foot's Bay, and Rosseau. Even more passengers invariably came aboard from Windermere House, the Royal Muskoka Hotel, and Clevelands House. The ship would then cruise to Natural Park, where everyone would disembark for a couple of hours to enjoy a delicious lunch, recline in the shade of an ancient tree, or meander along the walking trails. Eventually, the whistle would sound and passengers would climb aboard for the return trip. It made for a truly memorable excursion. When a 1953 Muskoka Lakes marketing brochure described the 100-Mile Cruise as "the most famous of its kind on the North American continent," it wasn't exaggerating.

Occasionally, unforeseen events would occur to make the cruise memorable in a more exhilarating way than intended. The most notable took place in the summer of 1951. The *Sagamo* had docked at Natural Park

Admiring a spectacular view of Mirror Lake from the bluffs in Natural Park.
Courtesy of Muskoka Boat and Heritage Centre.

Crew and passengers pose with *Sagamo* at Natural Park, 1927. Captain Lee stands in front of the officers on the right of the picture; to his right is famed musician Charles Musgrave, who led the orchestra aboard the 100-Mile Cruise.

Courtesy of Muskoka Boat and Heritage Centre.

and all the passengers were ashore, when suddenly, and without any warning, a freak storm blew in off the lake and began pushing the ship toward the beach. The pier to which *Sagamo* was moored was ripped from its cribbing and dragged along with it. To the startled witnesses onshore, it looked as though the massive vessel would be grounded and quite possibly holed. Luckily, a few of the crew were still onboard and reacted quickly to the impending disaster.

Did You Know?
The Muskoka Navigation Company fleet was the largest on any inland water system in Canada.

Captain Hill ordered engines brought to full reverse. At first their efforts seemed to make no difference; *Sagamo* continued to move toward the shore. Then, just as the onlookers thought the ship would be beached, she stopped and slowly began to back off.

Disaster had been averted by the quick actions of the crew, but with the wharf destroyed, there remained the dilemma of how to go about re-embarking the passengers. Captain Hill waited until the winds subsided, then gently brought the ship as close to the beach as possible and used small boats to ferry the passengers back aboard. The pier at Natural Park was quickly rebuilt and the 100-Mile Cruise continued as before with barely an interruption to its schedule.

The 100-Mile Cruise came to an abrupt end in 1958 when the final steamships of the company were retired. When that happened, Natural Park was suddenly without purpose. The tranquil property was sold and remains in private hands today, and all evidence of the park that awed passengers for nearly 40 years is now gone.

CHAPTER TEN

THE ROYAL MUSKOKA HOTEL

The late 1890s were full of optimism and ambition in Canada as the country recovered from a long depression. The Muskoka Lakes Navigation Company was thriving as never before. The holds of its steamships were packed full of all kinds of cargo and a seemingly endless line of passengers waited to board. The question on the minds of the shareholders was what could be done next to build on this success and bring in greater profits. What was the next logical step for the company?

The answer came in 1900 when a newcomer, Toronto lawyer E.L. Sawyer, appeared on the scene with a dynamic idea. Why not build a world-class hotel of its own to complement the steamer business? The idea was enthusiastically endorsed by the board of directors; there were already dozens of thriving resorts in Muskoka and all believed there was room for one more, especially if it set itself apart by incorporating the latest amenities. The Grand Trunk Railway also saw potential in the ambitious scheme and was brought in as a partner.

They briefly considered buying and upgrading an existing hotel, such as Monteith House in Rosseau, but in the end the company decided it was more cost-effective to build from the ground up. Wrenshall's Point, a picturesque point of land jutting out into Lake Rosseau and providing unmatched views, was purchased, and Lucius Boomer, the architect of the famous Waldorf Astoria in New York City, was brought on board to design the new hotel.

Construction got underway in early 1901 and the Royal Muskoka Hotel opened for business that summer, though it wouldn't be fully completed until the following year.

When finished, the Royal Muskoka Hotel was undeniably the largest and grandest summer resort in all of Muskoka, a strikingly beautiful property capable of accommodating 350 guests. The hotel had a great three-storey rotunda with stately staircases sweeping up to spacious balconies flanked by two towers and a pair of huge dormitory wings. Every possible amenity and comfort was provided for guests, including electric lighting, hot and cold running water, a post office, telegraph office, bar, billiard room, bakeshop, newsstand, barbershop, and beauty salon. The 130-acre grounds boasted a nine-hole watered golf course, bowling greens, tennis courts, riding stables, and miles of shaded walking trails. A carriage road ran down to the steamboat wharf, which included two-storey boathouses with swimming platforms and all manner of pleasure boats for hire. The Royal Muskoka set a new standard in sophistication for cottage country resorts.

Statesmen, politicians, millionaires, and even some European royalty flocked to the exciting new hotel, eager to enjoy its luxuries and a taste of the Canadian wilderness. Indeed, the hotel attracted such a steady stream of guests that the Muskoka Lakes Navigation Company was compelled to build a new steamer, *Sagamo*, to keep up with demand. Even so, and as incredible as it may seem, the hotel did not contribute as much to the company's coffers as expected. It was expensive to upkeep, required a large staff to cater to the wealthy in the manner to which

Postcard depicting the *Nipissing* docked at the Royal Muskoka Hotel on Lake Rosseau. The Royal, as the hotel was often simply called, was built and owned by the Muskoka Navigation Company and was, for its time, the most palatial resort in the region.
Courtesy of Ron Sclater.

This period postcard depicts the dining room of the Royal Muskoka Hotel. Politicians, royalty, Hollywood stars, and millionaire businessmen were at home in these elegant surroundings.
Courtesy of Ron Sclater.

they were accustomed, and the tourist season was short — three months at the most. As a result, even when the hotel was fully booked, it made only modest profits. Shareholders understandably feared any downturn in tourism.

Their worst fears were realized in 1929 when the stock market crashed, driving the world into the darkness of the Great Depression. The summer tourists all but disappeared; in fact, many times the staff outnumbered the names on the guest register. The sound of their footsteps echoing down cavernous, empty halls was a constant reminder for staff just how desperate the situation had become. Throughout the 1930s, merely keeping the hotel open swallowed up much of the profits earned by the steamers. There certainly wasn't any money available to make badly needed upgrades to a building that had grown somewhat dated, and as the decade wore on and neglect continued, it only grew more dilapidated, until the Royal Muskoka Hotel could no longer be considered an asset.

It was a welcome relief when guests began to return in the late 1930s, but by then the Royal Muskoka's best days were decades in the past. Anticipating a return to the glory days of a half-century before, the hotel was given an expensive and comprehensive overhaul in 1946. The results, however, were disappointing, and the hotel failed to attract enough business to make it profitable.

The owners struggled with the decision of what to do with the palatial resort. In the spring of 1952, shortly before the onset of the tourist season, the decision was taken out of their hands in dramatic fashion. At 2:00 a.m.

fire broke out in one of the hotel's dormitory wings and within minutes the flames flared up and consumed the great hotel. Flames reached hundreds of feet up into the night sky, creating a hellish glow that was visible miles away. Driven to the fire like moths to light, dozens of curious cottagers converged on the dying building. As the flames rose, some onlookers mourned the loss of the Royal Muskoka while others raced into the hotel to scavenge souvenirs. Within a few hours the fire had burned itself out, but not before completely destroying the building. By morning, all that remained were the chimneys, which poked up through the smouldering coals and shroud of smoke like the ribs of a massive skeleton.

Ronald Blackie was a youngster at the time of the fire but the event burned itself into his memory:

> Early in the morning of May 18, I awoke to see a glowing in the sky to the north, and learned from our neighbors that the Royal Muskoka Hotel had gone up in flames. Later in the morning, after the alleged rush of looters and gawkers, Dad and I took the boat up the lake for a look. There were not many people about, no officials, no yellow caution tape such as there would be today. We docked at the main hotel dock. Only ashes remained … some still smoldering. There was absolutely nothing left, but a glint caught my eye; I bent down and picked up a key, with its tag still attached, indicating it was the key to the hotel dining room. How this cardboard tag survived the conflagration is a mystery.[1]

The key Blackie is referring to is now part of the collection of the Muskoka Lakes Museum in Port Carling.

With the exception of this lone key, the destruction had been complete. Nothing could be salvaged from the rubble. There was never any thought of rebuilding — the cost would have been too great and the reward uncertain. Instead the land was subdivided for cottages and the Royal Muskoka Hotel, at one time Canada's most prestigious resort, slipped quietly into history.

CHAPTER ELEVEN

THE SEGWUN MUSEUM

Following the final, incident-filled sailing season of 1958, the last three Muskoka steamships — the once-proud *Sagamo*, *Cherokee*, and *Segwun* — lingered at the Gravenhurst dockyards, where they faced an uncertain future. Though some may have held out hope that one or more of the vessels would be saved, the reality was there would be no last-minute salvation. Their sailing days were over, and in 1959 the assets of the Muskoka Navigation Company, the three remaining steamships included, were sold to a pair of Gravenhurst entrepreneurs, George Morrison and Jack Vincent. They were really only interested in *Sagamo* — which they intended to turn into a floating nightclub and restaurant — and the former shipyards, which were to become a marina where *Sagamo* would be permanently moored.

The *Sagamo* was given a fresh coat of paint and decorated with nautical décor; the tables arranged cabaret-style in the upper lounge. Morrison and Vincent invested heavily in the ambitious scheme, installing $1,200 in modern restaurant equipment and advertising heavily to get the word out. There was considerable buzz in town about this exciting new entertainment and dining venue, but after a solid first season it soon became apparent the steamship would not enjoy a long and prosperous second career as the Sagamo Floating Restaurant. By 1963 the restaurant had closed and the once-majestic ship sat vacant and lifeless, appearing more and more dismal with each passing year as the owners debated her fate.

What of *Sagamo*'s sister ships? In 1960, after two years of languishing forlornly alongside the docks, *Cherokee* was scrapped and her engines removed for sale. No one quite knew what to do with *Segwun*. There were no buyers and no apparent commercial application. It seemed certain that she would eventually be cut up for scrap metal. But a group of Gravenhurst citizens who recognized her historic importance rode to *Segwun*'s rescue. They opened negotiations with the ship's owners, who generously agreed to sell her to the town for one dollar on the condition that the town would agree to preserve the vessel as a floating marine museum commemorating the faded steamship era in Muskoka. The offer was enthusiastically accepted.

Having sat idle and neglected for two years, *Segwun* was hardly fit for visitors. A lot of costly work would need to be done to get her ready for her new role. Fundraising efforts brought in $1,200, a figure matched by the town of Gravenhurst. The idea of a floating museum captured the imagination of many in town and there was no shortage of volunteers offering their services. So during the spring and summer of 1962, the weathered and wearied vessel was restored to a semblance of her former glory. A new coat of paint brightened her hull, brass fittings in the engine room were polished until they shone like mirrors, and windows that had been broken by vandals were replaced.

But although many of her original fittings remained, including the anchor, telegraph, flags, and lifeboats, much more in the way of artifacts would be required if the vessel were to serve as a museum. So a call for donations went out, and all summer long a steady stream of items of historic interest began pouring in, including old charts,

For more than a decade, throughout the 1960s and into the 1970s, *Segwun* floated alongside a dock in Gravenhurst as the Segwun Steamboat Museum. Many doubted the vessel would ever sail again.
Courtesy of Muskoka Boat and Heritage Centre.

black and white photographs, boarding tickets, and even uniforms. Portions of the freight desk were devoted to lumbering and railroad exhibits and the staterooms were converted into exhibit galleries for pictures, though two were kept exactly as they had appeared in the days of the Muskoka Lakes Navigation Company. Similarly, the galley and dining room were outfitted just as they were in sailing days, the tables coming from Royal Muskoka Hotel.

Work proceeded under the watchful eye of Alvin Saulter, former chief engineer of the company and the man nominated to serve as the museum's first curator.[1] There couldn't have been a better choice. Not only was he the source of many colourful anecdotes from a lifetime spent aboard ship, but he was passionately devoted to the steamships and made sure that the restoration was performed to the same high standards that he insisted upon among his former crew. Coming aboard on the morning of the museum's grand opening must have been an odd experience for Saulter. Because the restoration had been so faithfully completed, it must have looked to him as if *Segwun* might begin haloing her stack any moment, the horn signalling her departure.

While *Segwun* was not about to sail again, the opening ceremonies on August 4, 1962, were nonetheless a joyous occasion. A parade featuring a pipe band and vintage and modern fire trucks was led down to the wharf by Mayor Simmons and two MPs dressed in vintage frock coats and top hats. On the docks, hundreds of assembled onlookers shuffled restlessly as speeches were made by a number of dignitaries, including Mayor Simmons and Bryan Cathcart (Ontario's minister of travel and publicity). Finally, after what seemed like an eternity to the excited crowds, a ribbon suspended between *Segwun* and the nearby *Sagamo* was cut, proclaiming the museum officially opened. There was a roar of approval from the crowd as this new chapter in *Segwun*'s history began.

Supported by a small annual grant from the Ontario government, and another from the town of Gravenhurst, the Segwun Steamboat Museum served as one of Muskoka's premier tourist attractions. Open daily in July and August, and on weekends from Victoria Day through to Thanksgiving, an average of 70 to 120 visitors boarded every day. Over the ensuing decade the exhibits were expanded and refined, and on occasion former crew members, most regularly retired Captain Wesley Hill, who resided in Gravenhurst, would visit the museum to entertain guests with nautical tales.[2] Saulter retired as curator in 1970 and was replaced seamlessly by George Harvey, supported by a passionate museum board.[3] *Segwun*, everyone agreed, was once again a vibrant part of the Muskoka landscape.

For a brief time people thought that perhaps *Sagamo* might enjoy a revival. After five years of sitting abandoned and lifeless, in 1968 new buyers emerged with the intention of reopening her as a restaurant. Hastily revitalized, she opened that summer and enjoyed a successful first season. The owners had every right to look to the future with optimism. Unfortunately, their hopes were soon dashed, and in spectacular fashion. January 10, 1969, saw the couple repainting the dining room for the restaurant's second season, when suddenly the heater being used to dry the paint exploded, starting a fire. The fumes and fresh paint fed the flames, which soon raced through the hull from bow to stern. By the time the Gravenhurst Fire Department managed to put out the fire, the entire wooden superstructure was destroyed, leaving only a metal skeleton twisted by the intense heat. The smoke rising from the ashes carried with them any dream of *Sagamo* ever being revived. Her destruction was complete. *Segwun* was now well and truly alone — the last steamship on the Muskoka Lakes.

CHAPTER TWELVE

RESTORATION

While the Segwun Museum proved a popular attraction, by the late 1960s serious doubts began to emerge about the vessel's future. Close inspection revealed subtle but startling signs of decay. Corrosion was notable in the metal, while parts of the hurricane deck were growing spongy with rot. Most concerning was that the ship's hull had not been out of the water since 1955 and was badly pitted. No one had any idea just how badly the integrity of the hull had been compromised by years of sitting dockside, but it was a very real possible that she might begin to leak at any moment. After serving as a museum for 11 years, it was clear that *Segwun*'s days were numbered unless a major refit was undertaken.

It was long the dream of adoring observers and steamboat buffs that the old ship would come out of retirement and again sail the lakes that once knew her so well. The mission to restore the ship to its former self, or something resembling it, began to gain momentum once it was discovered to what extent the decay had set in on the ship. After all, it seemed pointless to spend large amounts of money on an old steamship just to see it sit in the water to begin rusting and rotting again. It was like putting a Band-Aid on a wound that would not heal. To some, the idea of having this vessel waste away as a museum seemed senseless because there was so much more potential for *Segwun* if restored to complete operating conditions. Sightseeing cruises, like those of old, could be offered; practical demonstrations of her machinery in action would be possible; and nostalgic visits to some of her old ports of call would be sure to stoke the public imagination. What about the appeal of an autumn cruise to take in the splendour of the fall foliage? The possibilities of a fully revived and functioning *Segwun* seemed limitless, but for years it remained little more than a fantasy.

The dream of a restored *Segwun* began to move into the realm of reality in 1969 when John Coulter, a marine engineer who had served on *Segwun* during his student days, returned to Gravenhurst to fulfill a promise he had made to himself ten years earlier: to undertake a restoration of the steamship so that it was every bit as majestic as it had been when he had been a member of her crew.

With no financing of his own, Coulter knew he had to sell his vision, and he began with meeting with Gravenhurst mayor Hugh A. Bishop. His passion and practical engineering knowledge quickly won Bishop over, and during the course of this meeting was born the Segwun Restoration Project. Others — historians, business leaders, local politicians, steam-enthusiasts, and craftsmen — also threw their support behind the project, many offering their time and expertise to make it a success.

But one hurdle remained before work could begin. Would the Department of Transportation allow a ship with a wooden superstructure to carry passengers? It was a very real concern, and if the answer proved to be no, there was little sense in proceeding with the costly restoration. Thankfully, government officials saw the value of the project and endorsed it, provided of course that stringent safety measures were met and the vessel passed inspection. It was all project organizers could ask for, and the way was clear for work to begin.

Segwun is pulled from the water before undergoing restoration. There was concern that the ship had rotted so badly during its decade of inactivity that it would be beyond salvation, but, fortunately, this was not the case.
Courtesy of Muskoka Boat and Heritage Centre.

The first step was to remove tons of dirt and debris from the ship's bilges in preparation for the inspections. At the same time, layers of paint that had built up over the years and which posed a serious fire hazard were stripped away. For the first time in decades it was possible to get an idea of the condition of the wood underneath, and what they found was rot far in excess of what was originally imagined.

Unfortunately, just as work got underway, a rift began to form between the Museum Board, who were doubtful that *Segwun* could ever sail again under her own power, and those who favoured restoring her. The debate grew particularly heated and the parties involved seemed unable to find any middle ground. To many on the board it did not seem possible that enough funds and expertise could be found for *Segwun* to ever sail under her own power again. It was far better, in their minds, to have the ship serve as a museum than to see her languish for years undergoing endless renovations. Finally, the relationship grew so acrimonious that in 1970 the Gravenhurst Town Council was put in the uncomfortable position of having to arbitrate a resolution. Enamoured with the upside of Coulter's vision, the council voted to allow restoration to proceed. Most members of the Museum Board resigned and a new Museum Committee composed of forward-thinking individuals was formed.

But a new opponent emerged to threaten the project: decay. Pinhole leaks were spreading in the hull, especially around the waterline, that threatened to sink *Segwun*. The old ship could not hold on much longer. It was a race against time. Money was the main hindrance; despite fundraising efforts and a promised grant of $12,000 from the Ontario government pending an inspection of the steamer's hull, there simply weren't enough funds for work to begin in earnest. Just as people began to despair, a saviour emerged: the Ontario Road Builders' Association (O.R.B.A.).

At first it seemed an unusual partnership, but the O.R.B.A. had good reason to be interested in the plight of *Segwun*. First, some of the association's executives were longtime cottagers in Muskoka and were familiar and passionate about the region's steamship history. In addition, the O.R.B.A. saw the project as a means of raising their public profile by assisting in a project that had heritage and cultural significance for a large part of the province.

Laying out their proposal, the O.R.B.A. offered to fully sponsor a complete refit of *Segwun*, with technical assistance from its 130 member companies. The association would obtain title to the ship and set up a new governing society to oversee the work and eventual operation of *Segwun*. Once the project was complete, the O.R.B.A. would relinquish its control of the ship and step aside.

Needless to say, the O.R.B.A.'s offer was gratefully accepted by *Segwun* Committee and the town of Gravenhurst. A new group called the Muskoka Steamship and Historical Society was organized.

Above: *Segwun* in dry dock during the restoration. She required a brand new bottom, two propeller shafts, and a new forepeak in addition to other costly repairs.
Courtesy of Muskoka Boat and Heritage Centre.

Left: New propeller shafts were installed aboard *Segwun* in May 1974.
Courtesy of Muskoka Boat and Heritage Centre.

Prime Minister Pierre Trudeau aboard *Segwun* for her re-launch ceremony, June 1, 1974. Despite this exciting event, it would be another six years before work was completed and the ship was ready to carry passengers.
Courtesy of Muskoka Boat and Heritage Centre.

With a steady flow of money, the project progressed steadily. On August 1, 1973, *Segwun* was pulled from the water and dry docked for the first time in decades. To no one's surprised, the entire hull-plating and the rudder had to be replaced. The $70,000 contract went to Collingwood Shipyards Ltd. and Herb Fraser and Associates of Port Colborne. In addition, two new propellers, costing $5,000 apiece and crafted from bronze, were ordered from Quebec. At the same time as outer-hull restoration got underway, superstructure repairs proceeded under the supervision of Fred Kruger, a master carpenter from Severn Bridge. Throughout 1973 and the following spring crews worked feverishly so that *Segwun* could be re-launched in the summer of 1974.

June 1, 1974 was a fittingly splendid summer day. As many as 6,000 people, including a number of dignitaries and former officers of the Muskoka Lakes Navigation Company (in full uniform), flocked to Muskoka Bay to witness the historic event. On hand was the prime minister of Canada, Pierre Elliott Trudeau, who addressed the crowd with a short but inspiring speech before breaking the customary bottle of champagne over the ship's hull. A cheer erupted from the crowd as the steamer slid back into the water. It was an exciting day and the public began to realize that a fully restored and operational *Segwun* was no longer just a dream, but was rapidly becoming a reality. Much more remained to be done, however.

Dozens of pleasure boats swarmed *Segwun* on the occasion of her re-launch to get a closer look.
Courtesy of Muskoka Boat and Heritage Centre.

Throughout 1974 the entire hurricane deck and the fore and aft sections of the promenade deck were rebuilt, the existing wood having badly rotted. Most of the new lumber had to be specially milled to look like the original. The exterior paint was burned off and new coats — six in total — of fire-retardant paint applied. In 1976 the boiler and all interior piping, which was partially corroded, were replaced or rebuilt. The all-important original steam engine, however, was left in its original condition for obvious historical reasons. The only exceptions were made for safety reasons, operating efficiency, or compliance with modern regulations.

Work slowed in 1977 when the government insisted that costly new watertight steel bulkheads would be required before *Segwun* would be certified for more than a mere 49 passengers, which meant a return to the drawing board and a search for new sources of funding. Thankfully, the Ontario Ministry of Industry and Tourism gave the project a morale-lifting boost in the form of a $400,000 grant, which allowed work to resume at a brisk pace in 1978.

By autumn of 1980, most of the work had been completed. The new *Segwun* was stronger, safer, and more comfortable, without having sacrificed any of her character. She no longer had her staterooms (overnight trips were banned due to the fire risk), but she otherwise appeared as she had during her heyday. Modern equipment, expertly disguised so as to not detract from the vintage atmosphere, included radar, depth sounder, life rafts, emergency backup diesel generators, and ship-to-shore radio.

It was now time for sea trials to begin. On October 7, *Segwun* backed away from the dock, swung her bow around, and tentatively sailed out onto Lake Muskoka for the first time in 22 years. It was to be a short jaunt, as problems developed in her port engine and necessitated a return to Gravenhurst on one propeller. More problems surfaced on the second day of trials, when once again the steamer was reduced to a single engine. After two days of rather disappointing tests, it became clear that more work had to be done on the temperamental engines. Unfortunately, the funds had run out. With the end in sight, it was a bitterly disappointing development.

A solution presented itself when it was decided that a new private company would be allowed raise the necessary funds and then lease and operate the vessel on behalf of the society. The new company — known as the Muskoka Lakes Navigation and Hotel Company — was managed by S. Gordon Phillips, an expert tourism planning consultant who had already spent seven successful years managing the cruise ship *Lord Selkirk* on Lake Winnipeg. Under his expert guidance, the company managed to raise $100,000. They completed all the work by the summer of 1981 — a brilliant achievement after the grim outlook of just a year before.

On June 21, 1981, *Segwun* completed a shakedown or test cruise through the locks at Port Carling and proceeded on to some of her old haunts, including Clevelands House and Windermere House. Everywhere she went, *Segwun* was escorted by a flotilla of boats and greeted by crowds of excited onlookers. Everyone was thrilled — *Segwun* was back!

CHAPTER THIRTEEN

THE RMS *SEGWUN* REBORN

June 27, 1981, was a historic day for Muskoka. It was the day when the steamship era on the Muskoka Lakes returned with the maiden voyage of the painstakingly restored RMS *Segwun*. On hand that glorious summer afternoon was the Honourable Frank Miller, then an MPP, but at one time the manager of the Muskoka Lakes Navigation Company. After a touching ceremony attended by a large number of curious onlookers, Miller officially cut the ribbon that ushered in the fourth stage in *Segwun*'s history. Public cruises were offered, starting that very afternoon.

During the first season back on the lakes, *Segwun* was commanded by Captain Clyde Mock of Owen Sound, a veteran Great Lakes officer with decades of experience (after two seasons, Mock was replaced by Captain Jim Caldwell, another experienced Great Lakes mariner who remained at the helm of the historic ship for the next 26 seasons). During that inaugural year, *Segwun* ran six days a week, usually on short cruises, but with two all-day trips to either Windermere House or Paignton House.[1] As the kinks in her machinery were ironed out and the crew became more comfortable handling a vessel whose technology was more than a century out of date, the company felt comfortable in expanding the excursions.

Centennial celebrations for *Segwun*. As many as 5,000 people were on hand for this important Muskoka event.
Courtesy of Muskoka Boat and Heritage Centre.

Segwun *on Film*

Segwun has become something of a movie star since its re-launch. Its first starring role came in 1986 during the filming of *The Boy in Blue*, a Nicolas Cage and Christopher Plummer film based on the life of world-famous Toronto sculler Ned Hanlan. *Segwun* can be seen frequently throughout the movie, giving the film the authentic feeling of the late 19th century.

In 2011 the vessel again took a lead role, this time in the CBC film *Sunshine Sketches of a Little Town*. In this retelling of the humorous literary classic written by Canadian author Stephen Leacock, *Segwun* stands in for the fictional steamship *Mariposa Belle*.

On June 27, 1983, *Segwun* made a triumphant return up the Muskoka River to Bracebridge, a community that had once served as *Segwun*'s home port. As many as 75 motorboats escorted her up the river, where more than a thousand people lined the shores of the harbour below the falls to give her a warm welcome. When the old lady finally slid gracefully into view, an excited chorus of applause and cheers erupted from the crowd. The voyage was such as success that *Segwun* repeated the trip five more times that summer. Unfortunately, the trip would not be repeated. Despite the obvious appeal of being tied to one of Muskoka's premier tourist attractions, the Bracebridge Town Council decided to go forward with a fixed, low-level bridge across the river below the town wharf, effectively shutting *Segwun* off from the community forever.

Even as *Segwun* enjoyed her successful revitalization, the company never forgot her sister ship that had met a tragic end. On October 6, 1984, a wreath was laid on the wreck of *Waome*, and on August 3, 1986, the fate of *Nipissing* was likewise commemorated at Port Cockburn. Both were touching ceremonies.

A more joyous celebration took place in 1987 to celebrate *Segwun*'s centennial year. The birthday party for the old ship was planned for July 4, and it was assumed the event would be met with some interest. But no one was prepared for the genuine outpouring of love for *Segwun* that took place that day, as more than 10,000 people swarmed into town for the festivities, a rare and spontaneous expression of affection that demonstrated just how beloved the historic steamship truly is.

Buoyed by the success of *Segwun*, in 2006 the town of Gravenhurst built the Muskoka Boat and Heritage Centre, a 20,000-square-foot state-of-the-art museum celebrating all that is uniquely wonderful about this area of Ontario. The Muskoka Steamship and Historical Society was chosen to operate it on their behalf. The centre includes interactive displays devoted to steamships, resorts, and lumbering. The facility is also home to Grace and Speed, North America's largest in-water exhibit of working antique boats.

During the late 1990s, increased demand for cruises had prompted the society to consider building a new, larger companion ship for *Segwun*. It was also in the back of everyone's minds that the venerable ship may not be around forever and a successor was clearly needed. The result was *Wenonah II*, a ship that manages to retain a Victorian-era charm while still including modern conveniences lacking in *Segwun* such as air conditioning, an onboard elevator, and oil-driven turbines. The *Wenonah II* towers over her older sister with additional decking for viewing pleasure and a 200-passenger capacity, double that of *Segwun*. Since her launch in 2002 she has been particularly popular for weddings, corporate events, and leisurely dinner cruises.

Around the same time, the heritage society also acquired and undertook the restoration of *Wanda III*, a century-old steam yacht that had been languishing in Dorset, where there had been talk of restoring her to her former grandeur. The *Wanda III* had been built in 1915 for Mrs. Timothy Eaton, widow of the founder of the Eaton's

The success of *Segwun* led Muskoka Steamships to launch her sister ship, *Wenonah II*. She was designed as a replica of an early 20th-century Muskoka steamship, but with all the modern amenities.
Courtesy of Muskoka Steamships.

Wanda III, which operates alongside *Wenonah II* and *Segwun*, was once the private yacht of Lady Eaton, widow of Eaton's founder Sir Timothy Eaton.
Courtesy of Muskoka Steamships.

Fall foliage cruises aboard *Segwun* are particularly popular. It's a great way to take in the painter's palette of colours that transform the Muskoka landscape each October.
Courtesy of Muskoka Steamships.

department store chain. Her engines were from a Royal Canadian Navy minesweeper and were incredibly powerful, capable of a sustained cruising speed of 24 miles per hour, a speed unheard of on the Muskoka Lakes in those days.[2]

Today, the Muskoka Steamship Association continues to operate all three vessels on behalf of the Muskoka Steamship and Historical Society. *Segwun* and *Wenonah II* are among Canada's foremost tourist attractions. Aboard these elegant vessels, whether during a short one-hour jaunt, and entire afternoon, or an evening-long sunset cruise, passengers can feel the stress of their lives fade away as they take in the breathtaking views. Whether relaxing on deck, soaking up some sun, savouring a drink or a fine meal, or wandering the decks, they can experience the atmosphere of a turn-of-the-century steamship and imagine what it was like to sail these same waters more than a hundred years ago.

While *Wenonah II* may be larger and represent the future of the Muskoka Lakes Navigation Company, it is still *Segwun* that captures the imagination and represents a vital link to the area's history. With her elegance and authentic charm, the RMS *Segwun* remains the undisputed "Queen of Muskoka."

Segwun Timeline

1887: *Nipissing II* is launched, the hull built of Welsh iron at shipyards in Clyde, Scotland. Its first route is from Gravenhurst to Port Cockburn.

1898: The wheelhouse is rebuilt and set on the hurricane deck, and paddlewheels are lowered to get better movement in the water. The catwalks around the stern are removed to make way for an much larger dining salon.

1907: Route is reduced to local trips around Lake Muskoka due to ship's aging machinery.

1914: The walking-beam breaks at Milford Bay and the ship has to be towed back to Gravenhurst by the *Islander*.

1914–24: Ship is moored at Gravenhurst dockyards, where it is sometimes used by the yard crews as sleeping quarters.

1924: *Nipissing II* is rebuilt. The ship receives a new engine and the paddlewheels are removed. Ship renamed *Segwun*.

1930: Two small state rooms and aft (back) lounge are added.

1930: The black hull is painted grey.

1939: The grey hull is painted green.

1945–47: Staterooms are added amidships and the back lounge is removed.

1958: *Segwun* strikes a shoal at Gull Rock, on Lake Muskoka, and ceases operations.

1960: The ship is put up for sale as scrap metal, but is purchased by the town of Gravenhurst.

1962–73: Houses a museum run by the town of Gravenhurst.

1973: Purchased by Ontario Roadbuilders Association for restoration. *Segwun* is pulled from the water and dry docked.

1974: On June 1, *Segwun* is officially re-launched by Prime Minister Pierre Elliott Trudeau. Work continues.

1976: The Ontario government donates $400,000 for restorations.

1977 Canada Post honours *Segwun* with a 36-cent commemorative stamp.

1980: Sea trials commence.

1981: July 1 is the first sailing day and celebration; MPP Frank Miller is on hand to cut the ribbon.

1982: In August, *Segwun*'s last trip to Bracebridge takes place.

1987: On July 4, the 100th anniversary of *Segwun* is celebrated; Lieutenant Governor Lincoln Alexander attends.

1994: Town of Gravenhurst presents Muskoka Steamships with an Outstanding Achievement Award for creating, maintaining, and promoting a unique international attraction.

2001–02: For two consecutive years, Attractions Canada recognizes the RMS *Segwun* as the Best Large Attraction in the Province of Ontario.

2012: Short sightseeing excursions as well as lunch and sunset dinner cruises are available aboard *Segwun* during the operating season (visit *segwun.com* for full details and schedules). On Saturday August 18, 2012, the 100-Mile Cruise will be recreated on the RMS *Segwun* as the ship departs from Gravenhurst and traces the original route of the SS *Sagamo* steamship. More than 100 other wooden boats will accompany the *Segwun* on her journey; the proceeds of the event will be donated to the Canadian Cancer Society.

Ships' Specifications

Steamer	Dates	Length (feet)	Beam (feet)	Draft (feet)	Speed (miles per hour)
Wenonah	1866–85	80	15	6	10
Waubamik	1869–76	41	8	3	10
Nipissing I	1871–86	115	18	6	14
Simcoe	1867–80	49	12	6	14
Rosseau	1879–1915	70	12	4	12
Muskoka	1881–90	94	18	5	8
Muskoka (after rebuild)	1891–1912	110	18	5	12
Lake Joseph	1881–98	52	10	4	12
Kenozha	1883–97	110	18	n/a	12
Kenozha (after rebuild)	1898–1918	126	18	n/a	12
Oriole	1886–1927	75	15	4.5	12
Nipissing II	1887–1925	125	21	6	14
Medora	1893–1902	123	25	8.5	12
Medora (after rebuild)	1903–40	143	26	8.5	12
Ahmic	1896–1902	61	13	4.6	12
Ahmic (after rebuild)	1903–51	80	15	4.6	12
Islander	1900–54	100	19	6	14
Charlie M	1897–1906	52	11	3	14
Charlie M (after rebuild)	1907–19	74	11	3	14
Sagamo	1906–69	152	29	7.4	n/a
Cherokee	1907–61	120	23	6	16
Constance	1898–99	65	18	4	n/a
Constance (after rebuild)	1900–38	82	18	4	n/a
Segwun (1925–present)		21	6	25	128
Mink/Waome	1927–34	78	17	10	n/a

Notes

Chapter 1: Laying the Foundations of Muskoka Steamboating

1. The *Emily May*, known as the "Queen of the Lake Simcoe Steamers," was built in 1861 on behalf of Captain Isaac May of Beaverton (who named the boat after his eldest daughter). The *Emily May* was a 500-passenger luxury sidewheeler measuring 154 feet long and 24 feet wide. Connecting with the train at Bell Ewart, she called at the east and west ports of Lake Simcoe on alternate days. In 1883, after 21 years of service, the once-majestic *Emily May* was abandoned and left to rot in the shallows of Bell Ewart.

Chapter 2: Alexander Cockburn

1. Tatley, *The Steamboat Era in the Muskokas Volume 1*, 280.

Chapter 3: *Nipissing II*

1. George Bailey was born in 1847, the son of a pioneering Bracebridge fur trader and mill owner. As a young man he had rowed or paddled all over the Muskoka Lakes, becoming intimately familiar with its many rocks, shoals, islands, and inlets. This knowledge was put to good use during his lengthy career as a steamboat captain, beginning in 1880, when he became skipper of the newly built tugboat *Rosseau*. He served 55 years with the Muskoka Lakes Navigation Company and rose in the ranks until he was named commodore of the line as master of *Sagamo*. He reluctantly retired at the end of the 1922 season at the age of 75, and died in 1938.

Chapter 5: Muskoka Wharf: Then and Now

1. James McCabe and his wife, Catherine, who most simply called "Mother McCabe," were prominent figures in the early history of Gravenhurst. Indeed, they are generally considered the community's first settlers. James was born in Scotland in 1815, and by 1861 he had settled in Gravenhurst, where he met the recently widowed Catherine Grant. McCabe owned two properties in Gravenhurst. One was on Muskoka Bay, where he constructed a wharf that became known as McCabe's Landing. The other was at the south end of Gravenhurst (likely opposite St. James Anglican Cemetery on Muskoka Road) where he ran a rustic one-room tavern. Records say it had a bar in one corner, a post office in another, a cookstove in a third corner, and a dining table in the last. Mother McCabe, we learned, served guests a thirst-quenching drink consisting of water, molasses, and vinegar — using her hands to stir the ingredients! The inn was sold in 1867 and the McCabes tried their hand at farming. There are no records of James after this, though he may have died in a Refuge House in Walkerton at the age of 87.

2. Files, Muskoka Boat and Heritage Centre.
3. Fraser, *History of Muskoka*, 68.
4. Tatley, *The Steamboat Era in the Muskokas Volume 1*, 85.

Chapter 8: The RMS *Segwun*

1. Captain A. Peter Larson was the second in his family to command a Muskoka Navigation Company ship. His father, Captain Hans Larson, had been skipper of *Muskoka* for many years before retiring in 1913. A.P. Larson joined the company in 1895. Prior to taking over *Segwun*, his most notable command was the *Islander*. Age and stress forced him to take a shore position in the early 1930s, ending almost four decades afloat.
2. The SS *Noronic* was among the worst nautical disasters in Canadian history. Built in 1913 for the Canadian Steamships Line, she was the largest and most beautiful ship on the Great Lakes. She carried 600 passengers and 200 crew members. On the night of September 16, 1949, while docked in Toronto harbour, she had over 500 passengers aboard when fire broke out. By the time the flames had burned themselves out, *Noronic* was a blackened wreck and between 118 and 130 people were dead (records vary).
3. Jack Ariss was a lifelong mariner who spent 20 years as skipper of *Segwun*. On Labour Day 1956, the 69-year-old suffered a massive stroke aboard. He returned as nominal captain for a few cruises in 1957 but he served more as an adviser than a real skipper.

Chapter 9: The 100-Mile Cruise

1. Ralph W. Lee served aboard the ships of the Muskoka Lakes Navigation Company for almost six decades — an incredible run. His first sailing season was in 1891 at the age of only 20. He rose steadily through the ranks, and by 1907 was given command of *Muskoka*. Lee was captaining *Kenozha* when it caught fire during the night of August 15, 1918. He and the purser, asleep in the bridge cabins, barely escaped the flames by jumping over the side, leaving behind clothes and personal belongings.

   Lee was not found at fault for the fire that claimed the vessel, and was made the second master of *Sagamo* in 1923, a position that came with the honorary title of commodore. Some say the promotion made him imperious and pompous, earning him the nickname "Admiral." Regardless, Lee was a skilled mariner and was credited with saving five people from drowning over the course of his career. He retired due to ill health in 1945 and died 12 years later in Toronto.

2. A well-known Canadian musician, band leader, and music publisher of the early 20th century, Charles E. Musgrave was born in England in 1875. By 1909 he was living in Toronto, where he owned and operated Musgrave Bros., a Yonge Street music store, with his brother George Musgrave as partner. The store operated under a variety of names until 1933.

   Charles Musgrave wrote and published over 50 songs in his career, many of the more famous being patriotic tunes written during the First World War. Musgrave spent most summers vacationing in the Port Carling area and would often spend his evenings playing piano at various Muskoka resorts. Starting in 1923, he entertained guests aboard *Sagamo*. Musgrave died in 1953.

Chapter 10: The Royal Muskoka Hotel

1. Muskoka Lakes Museum exhibit.

Chapter 11: The Segwun Museum

1. Alvin Saulter spent most of his life around steam engines, both on land and on water. He began his career with the

Huntsville Navigation Company as a 19-year-old fireman aboard the *Joe* in 1918. Saulter worked aboard various vessels — most notably as chief engineer aboard *Iroquois* — and on the trains of the Portage Railway. In 1930, he was hired by the Muskoka Lakes Navigation Company. He served aboard *Segwun*, *Cherokee*, and finally *Sagamo*. Saulter had the good fortune of being one of the survivors of the ill-fated *Waome*, which sank on October 6, 1934.

2. Captain Wesley David Hill began his five decades as a ship's skipper as captain of the supply steamer *Alporto*. For many years he captained *Ahmic*, then *Islander*, and finally, during the late 1940s, *Sagamo*. He left the failing Muskoka Lakes Navigation Company in 1952 and wound up his career as captain of the *Bigwin* on Lake of Bays. He died in Gravenhurst in 1970.

3. George Harvey, the second curator of the Segwun Steamship Museum, had a bond with his predecessor that could only be forged in the fires of a shared traumatic experience. He, like Alvin Saulter, was serving as ship's purser aboard *Waome* when she sank in 1934.

Chapter 13: The RMS *Segwun* Reborn

1. Paignton House, which thrived for more than a century, has been replaced by The Rosseau, a J.W. Marriott Resort. It is arguably the most refined hotel in Muskoka.

2. The *Wanda III* has a length of 94 feet and a beam of only 12, allowing her to cut through the water like an arrow. She transported her owners to the Eaton Estate, Kawandag, near Rosseau, for many years. Despite her elegance and speed, she fell out of favour dramatically and suddenly. Around 1927, a young girl in Rosseau developed acute appendicitis, but despite the yacht's renowned swiftness the child did not reach the hospital in Bracebridge in time and she died onboard. The Eatons could not forget what had happened, however, and they ended up selling the boat shortly afterward.

SOURCES

Boyer, Barbaranne. *Grand Hotels of Muskoka*. Erin, ON: Boston Mills Press, 1987.

Boyer, Robert. *A Good Town Grew Here*. Bracebridge, ON: 1978.

Canadian Summer Resorts: Illustrated Souvenir and Guide. Toronto: F. Smith, 1900.

Cockburn, Alexander Peter. *To the Shareholders of the Muskoka and Georgian Bay Navigation Company*, 1902.

Coombe, Geraldine. *Muskoka Past and Present*. Toronto: McGraw-Hill Ryerson, 1976.

Duke, A.H., and W.M. Gray. *The Boatbuilders of Muskoka*. Erin, ON: Boston Mills Press, 1992.

Fraser, Captain Levi. *History of Muskoka*. Bracebridge, ON: self-published, 1946.

Hind, Andrew, and Maria Da Silva. *Muskoka Resorts: Then and Now*. Toronto: Dundurn, 2011.

Muskoka Boat and Heritage Centre files (various).

Pryke, Susan. *Explore Muskoka*. Erin, ON: Boston Mills Press, 1987.

Tatley, Richard. *The Steamboat Era in the Muskokas Volume 1 — To the Golden Years*. Toronto: Stoddart Publishing Company, 1983.

———. *The Steamboat Era in the Muskokas Volume 2 — The Golden Years to the Present*. Toronto: Stoddart Publishing Company, 1984.

———. *The Story of the Segwun*. Gravenhurst, ON: Muskoka Steamship and Historical Society, 1981.

Taylor, Cameron. *Enchanted Summers*. Toronto: Lynx Images, 1997.

Thomas, Redmond. "The Beginning of Navigation and the Tourist Industry in Muskoka." *Ontario History, Volume XLII*. Toronto: Ontario Historical Society, 1950.

Newspapers
Bracebridge Herald
Bracebridge Herald-Gazette
Gravenhurst Banner
Muskoka Sun

INDEX

(N.B. Illustrations are indicated by italics.)

ABOUT THE AUTHORS

Andrew Hind and Maria Da Silva are freelance writers who live in Bradford, Ontario. They specialize in history and travel, particularly that of Muskoka, a region they've come to intimately know and love. Both cottage in the region and have spent years exploring it while writing for a number of local publications. They contribute regular features to *Muskoka Magazine*, and their work can also be seen in the pages of other regional newspapers and magazines, such as *The Muskokan, Muskoka Life, Muskoka Sideroads*, and *Parry Sound Sideroads*. Beyond Muskoka, Andrew and Maria's articles have appeared in a host of national and international publications, among them the *Toronto Star, Horizons, Lakeland Boating*, and the *Globe and Mail*.

RMS Segwun: Queen of Muskoka represents Andrew and Maria's tenth book. Previous books include *Ghost Towns of Muskoka* (Dundurn, 2008), which examines the tragic history of a collection of communities from across Muskoka whose stars have long since faded, *Ghosts of Niagara-on-the-Lake* (Dundurn, 2009), in which the haunted heritage of this charming and historic community is explored, and *Muskoka Resorts: Then and Now* (Dundurn, 2011), which explores in-depth the history and charm of a dozen classic resorts from across the region. Some of their other titles include *Niagara: Daredevils, Danger, and Unforgettable Stories* (Folklore Publishing, 2009), *Secrets of Lake Simcoe* (James Lorimer, 2010), and *Cottage Country Ghosts* (Ghost House Books, 2010).

Together, Andrew and Maria host historical and paranormal guided tours, which aim to bring history alive in an intimate, tangible fashion. They can be reached at *maelstrom@symopatico.ca* or *dasilvababy@hotmail.com*.